"*GOD IS*, by Rev. Phil Strom is a gift to all spiritual seekers. I found it a most helpful supplement to my own recovery from addiction, and it emboldened my commitment to pursuit of Spirit while illuminating my spiritual path. Regardless of one's past history or religious tradition, *GOD IS* demonstrates human connection to the higher self and the loving, forgiving Divine in simple terms and in stories which will resonate with many."

—John Bray-Morris M.D.

"Rev. Phil once told me that we come into this world to identify our karma, and live through it in service, that we create our reality, and the rest is scenery.
He was right, you know."

—Donathan Heimbecker, author of
The Youngest Witness, a Memoir of Innocence and Retribution

"Rev. Phil shares his journey of finding a spiritual solution to his disease of drug addiction… He also shares some of the teachings he has learned from spiritual masters through the ages as well as how the 12 steps provided him with the tools and foundation to find recovery. The 12 step programs of AA and then NA gave him a fellowship of like-minded travelers on his journey…
Today he seeks to share his recovery and his experience, strength and hope with addicts who are struggling with the disease of addiction.
In *God Is*, Rev. Phil shares his core message of seeking a spiritual consciousness and finding the God of your understanding …
In a paradoxical journey, he finds the solution to his addictions in finding God…"

—Steven Lustbader, M.D.

"Rev. Phil, a friend and fellow pilgrim for nearly 20 years, has written a remarkable and courageous book. It turns out that *God Is: And I Thought It Was All About Me*, is really about us. It tells a story about a path so many of us have tread each in our own way and in our own experience from darkness to light, from suffering to redemption. Rev. Phil's authentic honesty documents his walk through the dark night of the soul into the light of new life. Rev. Phil understands the power of grace and the presence of God in his life and shares it for us as a gift for our journey of self-discovery into the life of God in our lives."

—Rev. Dr. Richard W. Murphy, Episcopal Priest

"No matter where you are in your life's journey...a struggle, a fall, recovery, or a lull - this candid story by Rev. Phil will speak to you. *GOD IS* shows us how the presence of the Divine is with us at all times and how we can transform in spite of all odds. Read it now!"

—Shubhraji, author of
In the Lotus of the Heart: The Essence of Relationships
Founder, Namah Vedanta Center, Woodstock, NY

GOD IS

THE GOD TRILOGY

BOOK 1 – GOD IS
coming soon:
BOOK 2 – GOD REALIZATION
BOOK 3 – GOD HEALS

THE COMPANION TO THE GOD TRILOGY

GOD SPEAKS

GOD IS

And I Thought It Was All About Me

The Gospel
of
Rev. Phil

A Spiritual Autobiography

The God Trilogy — Book 1

Rev. Philip Strom

© January, 2015

Church of the One God

GOD IS: *And I Thought It Was All About Me*

Published 2019 by Reverend Philip Strom
Church of the One God
1503 Llano Street, Suite A-4
Santa Fe, NM 87505
www.churchoftheonegod.org

Copyright © January 2015 by Reverend Philip Strom

All rights reserved. No part of this publication, including images, illustrations and artwork, except for brief quotations embodied in reviews or for other noncommercial uses permitted by copyright law, may be reproduced, stored in retrieval systems, distributed, or transmitted in any form or by any means — electronic, mechanical, photocopying, recording, or otherwise — without written permission of the publisher. Permission requests should be sent to the author at revphil@churchoftheonegod.org

First edition 2016 by Church of the One God
Printed in the United States of America

Second edition 2019 by Church of the One God

Library of Congress Control Number: 2018964473

ISBN-13:   978-0-9989524-0-6 (Regular Print/Paperback)
          978-0-9989524-1-3 (Large Print/Paperback)
          978-0-9989524-2-0 (eBook/Kindle)
          978-0-9989524-3-7 (eBook/Epub)

Editors: Lauren Gdovin and Linda J. Miller
Cover and Layout Design: Dree Morin, Dreemer Designs
           www.dreemerdesigns.com
Contributing Artist/Artwork: Linda J. Miller/Heart Chakra
Augmented Reality Technology: RealityX2
           https://www.realityx2.com

Contents

PRELUDE	ix
THE STORY OF REV. PHIL AND CHURCH OF THE ONE GOD	x
AUTHOR'S NOTE	xvi
The Twelve Steps	xvii
GOD IS	1
GENESIS	7
Part 1	7
Part 2	16
KARMA IS	19
Day-To-Day Karma	20
Life-To-Life Karma	21
Group Karma	24
GRACE IS	25
I WAS	27
SANCTUARY WAS	35
RICH WAS	38
CYNTHIA WAS	47
TERI WAS	55
Teri And The Reverend	59
Teri And Edgar Cayce	61
Teri And The Tarot	63
Teri And Recovery	67
GOD'S IN CHARGE	72
God's In Charge, If We Surrender	72
God's In Charge, Even If We Don't Surrender	78

MAULANA ZAINULABEDIN-KAZMI IS   86
    Maulana In Augmented Reality   86
    Maulana And My Heart   90
    Maulana And My Master   94
    Maulana On Charity   96
    Maulana On Mercy   97
    Maulana On True Spirituality   98

MARK AND THE RADIO   100

MY RADIO DHARMA   103
    God, September 11, 2001 And My Radio Dharma   103
    My Radio Dharma, The Next Phase: Television   107
    My Radio Dharma, The Ongoing Saga: A Radio Station   108

EMANUEL SWEDENBORG, EDGAR CAYCE, VAISHALI, LINDA DRAKE AND ME   112

A DEMONSTRATION OF UNCONDITIONAL LOVE: A SOUL MATE FOR ALL TIME AND SPACE   121

THE GOSPEL OF REV. PHIL   129
    IAI   131
    IAI - The Practice   132

REVELATION   135

THE GOD TRILOGY   137

THE COMPANION TO THE GOD TRILOGY   139

PRELUDE

On this Guru Purnima day I do not intend to give you any Ashtaakshari (eight letter) or Panchaakshari (five-letter) mantra based on any particular deity's name. Nor am I enjoining you to study any Upanishad, or the Gita or the Brahma Sutras. There is a simple five-letter pronouncement **"GOD IS"** ("Devudunnaadu," in Telugu). Make this your sheet anchor. If you go on reciting it, thinking over it, acting up to it and conveying it to others, immersing yourself in the bliss of this experience, you will be making the greatest contribution to the welfare of the world. Consider this mantra as the message for this Guru Purnima and proclaim it in all circumstances and at all places with all the conviction and strength you can command. The world can be turned into an earthly paradise if you strengthen your faith in God and demonstrate it in your actions. You must have the courage and determination to face any kind of problems and difficulties. By propagating this mantra you can promote the love of God and the fear of sin among the people. The mantra **"GOD IS"** can be more powerful than a mantra based on any particular deity's name.

From today, develop your faith in God; engage yourselves in dedicated service to society and make your lives purposeful and helpful to those in distress or need. Remember that whomsoever you may serve, you are serving God. This is my benediction for all of you.

Divine Discourse delivered by Bhagawan Sri Sathya Sai Baba on July 21, 1986

THE STORY OF REV. PHIL AND CHURCH OF THE ONE GOD

I am Reverend Philip Strom, the Spiritual Director for Church of the One God and am both an Ordained Transdenominational, Interfaith, Non-Congregational Minister and a State of New Mexico Licensed Alcohol Drug Abuse Counselor.

These two credentials were both made possible because of my engagement in a Twelve Step recovery program that helped me address and place in remission my drug addiction problems. With God's blessing and my continued involvement in my own recovery, I have not found the need to take any mood and/or mind altering substances since August 17, 1987. During my time in recovery I have seen how the spiritual principles that the Twelve Steps are based upon and encourage change, not only my life but the lives of countless other individuals who actively participate in the program.

My ordination means that I honor all paths that lead to the unknowable Supreme Consciousness. It is my belief that all things in and of this universe are creations of and are at one with the Creator. Like human children being placed in a school by their parents, as children of God, our souls choose to be placed on this dimensional school plane called Earth, always with the approval of Divine Love and Wisdom. We are here to learn certain lessons that once learned will allow us to create a Heaven on Earth and function as the equal of our Creator. My mission is to help facilitate this by teaching spirituality to anyone who requests it.

In 1997 I was a working as a counselor at a State of New Mexico-funded adolescent treatment center in Santa Fe, named La Nueva Vida (LNV). LNV was an eight- to ten-month residential program for both male and female adolescents diagnosed as Level II (substance abusers). Managed Care came to New Mexico and LNV was reassigned as a Level III (mental health problems) two- to three-week program, with the possibility of a renewal period of an additional two to three weeks.

This change made two things extremely clear to me. The first was that I was no longer going to be a counselor. My job would become a combination babysitter, chauffeur and police officer. The second was that the adolescents and their families, particularly from middle class or lower class, were not going to be serviced as they had been, which would create a great deal of suffering. I stayed at LNV long enough to graduate my clients and then I resigned.

During the end times I had numerous conversations, with my wife Lin and trusted friends, regarding what my focus for the future should be. It was suggested that I open a treatment center of my own. I rejected that idea for two reasons. The first reason was that the treatment center would be subjected to State of New Mexico oversight, by the same agencies that created the dysfunction I was attempting to get away from. The second reason was that I would wind up in a management role which would take me away from what I thought was my gift and purpose, counseling.

The outcome of these conversations was that I decided to become an ordained minister, open a counseling office and provide spiritual counseling on a donation basis. The concept of becoming an ordained minister was extremely appealing on two fronts. The first front being my belief that Twelve Step spirituality was producing better outcomes than the traditional therapeutic modalities the State was mandating to be used. The second front was that as a Minister I was, for the most part, protected from government interference in my practice by the First Amendment which separates church and state.

I embarked on the twin missions of becoming an Ordained Minister and founding an umbrella organization for my ministry. I received my ordination on September 15, 1997 from the New Mexico Theological Seminary. Church of the One God met the requirements for obtaining tax-exempt 501(c)(3) status as a religious charitable organization from the Internal Revenue Service and temporary exemption was granted on August 27, 1998 and made permanent on January 29, 2003.

I was initially going to name the organization Church of the Twelfth Step because of the transformative power I experienced from working the Twelve Steps. I backed off from that name because I believed it would violate the Traditions that guide Twelve Step fellowships and would create confusion as to who I was and what I did. I was then inspired to name the organization the name it carries to this day, Church of the One God. This name reflects the lessons I absorbed in my studies. I came to believe that all religions were designed to take the follower to the same destination. The religions differed in ritual and dogma but the further one advanced in the religion the more the religion was indistinguishable from any other. For a more in-depth of this concept check out Aldous Huxley's *The Perennial Philosophy*.

With the help of my beautiful and talented wife, Lin, the first Church of the One God logo, seen below, was created.

In 1999, again with Lin's help, the second rendition of the Church of the One God logo, seen below, was created. Not only were the symbols changed but they were sequenced to reflect my understanding of the ages, from oldest to youngest, left to right, of the religions they represented.

In the latter part of 2003, with Lin's assistance, the third and current version of the Church of the One God logo, seen below, was created. The logo was, in early 2015 graphically cleaned up and enhanced by my website designer and graphic designer, Dree Morin, https://www.dreemerdesigns.com

The individual symbols and their meaning are shown on the following pages.

Om is the symbol for the Hindu religion. Though it is used in other religions such as Buddhism, Jainism, and Sikhism, its first appearance is in the Vedanta texts titled the Vedas. It has many interpretations. The one I favor is that it represents the sound of Brahman (God) coming into existence.

The above is the Chinese symbol for the Tao, representing the religion of Taoism. The word Tao translates to "The Way" or to quote Wikipedia "it denotes the principle that is both the source, pattern, and substance of everything that exists."

The Star of David is a symbol of Judaism, representing the Jewish religion. It is believed that this symbol was on a magic shield owned by King David and that it protected him from his enemies. This symbol also appears on the flag of Israel.

The religion of Buddhism utilizes numerous configurations of The Buddha. The one above is known as Calling the Earth to Witness, and it represents the moment Buddha obtained enlightenment.

The cross, the most familiar symbol of the Christian religion, comes in a variety of configurations and styles. The one above is known as the Latin Cross. Though it might be the most widely recognized religious symbol, the origins of the Cross predate the Christian adaptation.

The Islamic religion is represented by the above written Arabic calligraphy symbol which represents the name Allah. In the Abrahamic religions Allah is the word for God. The most common meaning in the English language generally refers to the God of the Islamic religion. The name Allah is believed to be derived from the word al-ilāh, which means "the god", and is related to the names El and Elah, the Hebrew and Aramaic words for God.

AUTHOR'S NOTE

Blessings & Greetings,

For reasons that will become obvious, I must open this book with the following disclaimer: names have sometimes been changed to protect the anonymity of the parties involved, and the occurrences described are my best recollections, and they may not match the recollections of others involved.

I am writing this book for a number of reasons. The first is to introduce to you an all-powerful, all-knowing, ever-present, unconditionally-loving, non-judging Divine Presence that wants nothing but, and works for, your greatest good to be made manifest in your life. The second is to let you know that no matter how dysfunctional life starts out, no matter how destructive you are to yourself and/or abusive you are to others, you are never without the possibility of transformation. The final reason is to provide you with understandings and tools to facilitate that transformation.

I write this book not as a speculator or as a spectator; I write about my experiences. I present this book as a gift to you, just as the spiritual experiences I share with you were gifted to me. I believe in being of selfless service to my fellow spiritual beings. I believe each and every religion, theology and spiritual practice points its practitioners in that direction. As is heard very frequently in the rooms of Twelve Step fellowships, "You keep what you have by giving it away." Allow me to expand on that by stating, "You enhance what you have by giving it away."

May LOVE and LIGHT always guide you on your path.

The Twelve Steps

Throughout the book I make reference to my being informed by my working of several of the Steps of what is, in total, a Twelve Step program. In order for those of you who are not Twelve Steppers to have a context for a Twelve Step program, I am providing you with the official version of them, as copied from Alcoholics Anonymous' website (https://www.aa.org). My listing of Alcoholics Anonymous' Twelve Steps is not meant to be interpreted as an endorsement of them or to imply that these are the steps I reference as being worked. I have chosen to list this version of the Twelve Steps as an acknowledgment to their being the original Twelve Steps created. Since their creation, numerous Twelve Step programs have come into existence; each modifying the Twelve Steps, with permission from Alcoholics Anonymous, to reflect their own particular application.

Service Material from the General Service Office:
The Twelve Steps of Alcoholics Anonymous

1. We admitted we were powerless over alcohol—that our lives had become unmanageable.
2. Came to believe that a Power greater than ourselves could restore us to sanity.
3. Made a decision to turn our will and our lives over to the care of God as we understood Him.
4. Made a searching and fearless moral inventory of ourselves.
5. Admitted to God, to ourselves, and to another human being the exact nature of our wrongs.
6. Were entirely ready to have God remove all these defects of character.
7. Humbly asked Him to remove our shortcomings.
8. Made a list of all persons we had harmed, and became willing to make amends to them all.
9. Made direct amends to such people wherever possible, except when to do so would injure them or others.
10. Continued to take personal inventory and when we were wrong promptly admitted it.
11. Sought through prayer and meditation to improve our conscious contact with God, as we understood Him, praying only for knowledge of His will for us and the power to carry that out.
12. Having had a spiritual awakening as the result of these Steps, we tried to carry this message to alcoholics, and to practice these principles in all our affairs.

Copyright © 1952, 1953, 1981 by Alcoholics Anonymous Publishing (now known as Alcoholics Anonymous World Services, Inc.) All rights reserved. Rev.6/4/12 SM F-121

GOD IS

The first time I heard Jeffrey, the gentleman who is currently my Twelve Step sponsor, speak he summed up my being a drug addict in the following statement: "We don't do poisonous quantities of dangerous chemicals because we're happy." To further qualify that statement, I've come to believe that, "We don't do poisonous quantities of dangerous chemicals because we are spiritually connected." We do them because we are unhappy and spiritually disconnected. I've had the blessing of living in a lot of fear and pain and in not even knowing what Spirit was or that I had any connection with it or God. I believe drugs can bring you to a bottom more convincingly than any other behavior. The vast majority of people in the world suffer from unhappiness and disconnectedness but their dissociative behaviors rarely bring them to a bottom that drugs can, therefore, denying them the experience and the gift of hitting a bottom that affords them the opportunity to really look at their lives. Once we get to a place where we can no longer continue following self-will the only will that is left to us is God's will.

From the earliest of times, humankind has been searching for answers to four questions and all of the religions since then have attempted to answer them. The four questions are:

1. Who am I?
2. Where did I come from?
3. Why am I here?
4. Where am I going?

We have been asking these questions because the spirit within has been trying to refocus us on what we are here for. What we are here for is to learn the answer to these questions and then demonstrate that answer in our day to day lives. The answer is **GOD IS**. **GOD IS** who I am. **GOD IS** where I came from. To learn **GOD IS**, is why I am here. **GOD IS** where I am going.

What I am going to attempt to do is explore and explain why so simple an answer has, for the most part, eluded us for all these millennia. I will do this in the context of an autobiography but first I'd like to express some of my beliefs. And even before we list a belief, let us define the word. Belief is, according to WordWeb, "any cognitive content held as true." According to Merriam-Webster's Online Dictionary belief means "conviction of the truth of some statement or the reality of some being or phenomenon especially when based on examination of evidence." The power of our beliefs is immeasurable. The Second Step in the Twelve Step program (Copyright 2008 Alcoholics Anonymous World Services, Inc.) sets the foundation of the practitioner's individual recovery by asking them to "Come to believe that a Power Greater than ourselves could restore us to sanity." The Law of Karma teaches us that what we do, what we think, what we feel, and what we believe is made manifest in our lives.

I believe **GOD IS**. What that means is that there is nothing that isn't God. We will continue to use the word God, along with other synonyms, for convenience sake. If you object to this word feel free to substitute your own word as you read. Just remember, we are defining a belief, not an entity or being or form of energy and/or intelligence. As the Tao Te Ching (written by Lao Tzu and translated by Stephen Mitchell, chapter 1) teaches us, "The Tao that can be told is not the eternal Tao. The name that can be named is not the eternal name. The unnameable is the eternally real. Naming is the origin of all particular things."

My sub-belief expands beyond the simple, all-encompassing **GOD IS** because at the beginning of the path the sub-beliefs, however redundant they may be, serve to further our demonstrations. My first sub-beliefs are that **GOD IS** perfect and that everything, including all Souls, were created by God in the very first moment of creation and nothing new has been created since. Therefore, if **GOD IS** perfect and God created everything, everything has to be whole and everything has to be perfect. What that means is that there cannot be any polarity in God's universe. However, while in human form we perceive almost everything as polarized (also known as duality): male/female, good/bad, positive/negative, optimistic/pessimistic, etc. This contradiction is the reason we are in this form.

My next sub-belief is that since we are all created by the Creator, we have the powers of creation. This can take many forms from creating a new life with the participation of another human being of the opposite gender, to creating our own reality by what we do, think, feel and believe (karma), to creating one substance out of another substance, as demonstrated by Jesus when he turned water into wine (the Gospel According to Saint John, the *King James Version*, Chapter 2, Verse 9) and to the ultimate act of creation, turning a human being into a purely spiritual being (Buddha's nirvana and Jesus' resurrection).

This leads to the sub-belief that all of God's human creations have free will. It is this free will that we are here to learn how to use in a manner that moves us closer to reunification with God as opposed to further away from it. That is the lesson that leads to the answer of the third question and the destination in the fourth question. Because we are one with the Creator we were in need of a real powerful teacher to show us the folly of following self-will instead of God's will. To carry out this task, another sub-belief, God created Ego as free-will's master teacher. It is our Ego that creates the duality in this plane of human existence. And since God created Ego, Ego does its job, as all other of God's creations do, perfectly.

Below is a diagram of a neutral Free Will. Life presents a stimulus and both Spirit and Ego interpret the stimulus and suggest a course of action to Free Will. Free Will makes a determination as to a response choosing either Ego's or God's Will's recommendation or some combination of both. Free Will sends the determination to Mind which then generates Action based upon the determination.

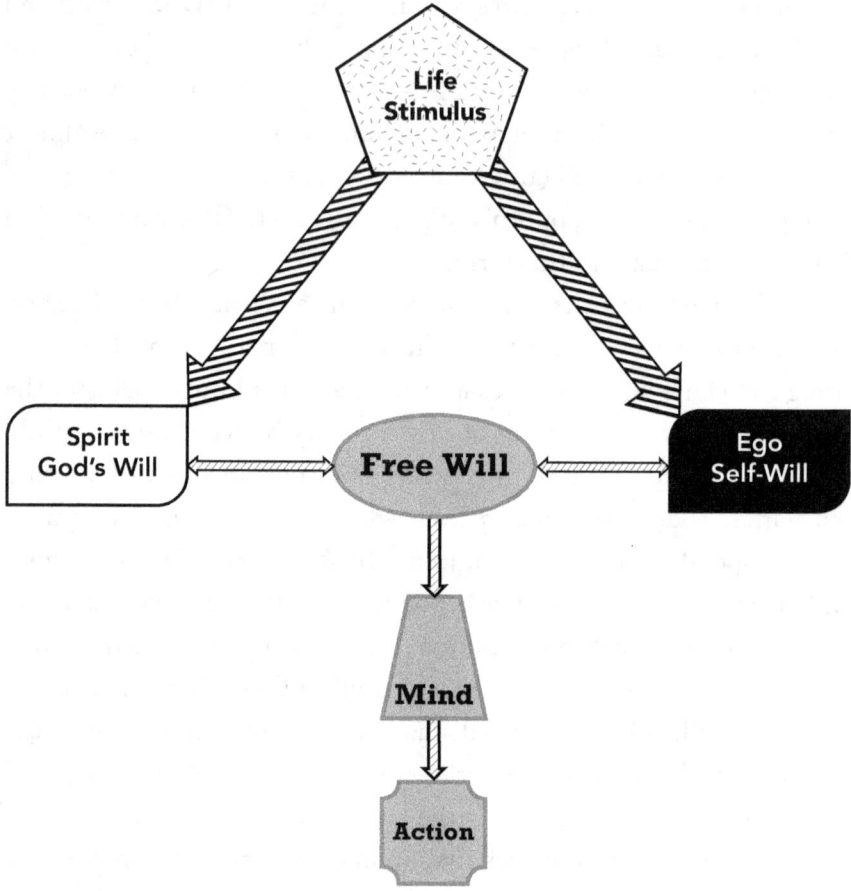

When we choose Ego regularly our Free Will becomes colored with that determination, as pictured below.

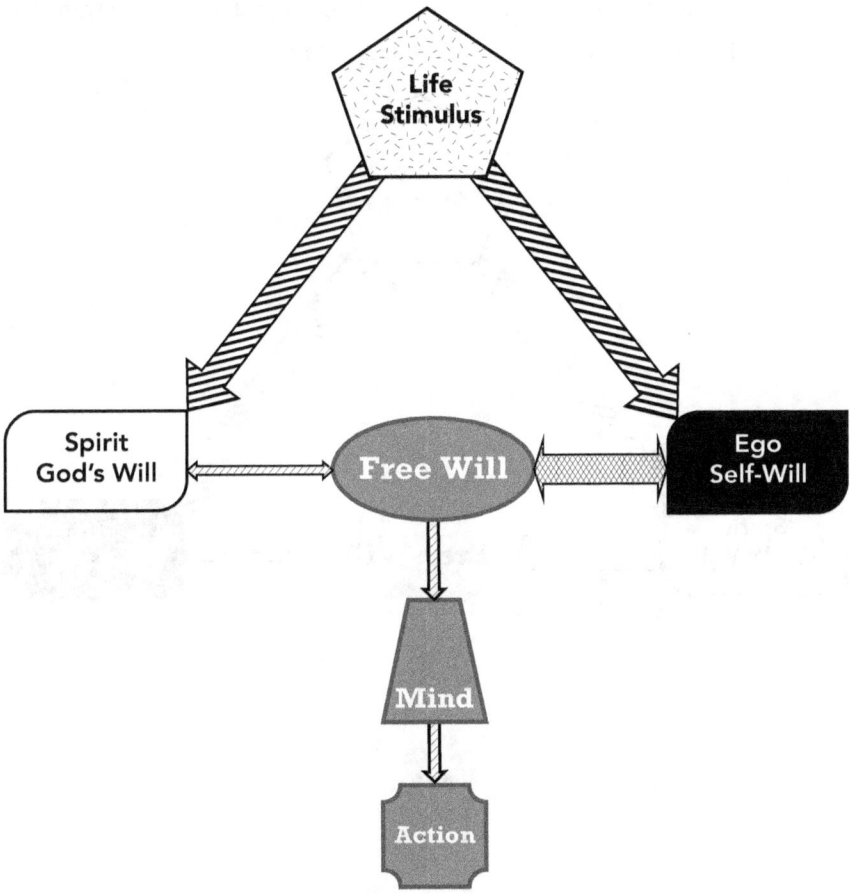

The more Free Will chooses Ego the harder it becomes to choose Spirit. Harder doesn't mean impossible. To change it requires us to meditate, pray and stay in the moment. Doing this will change the coloring from dark to light, as pictured below.

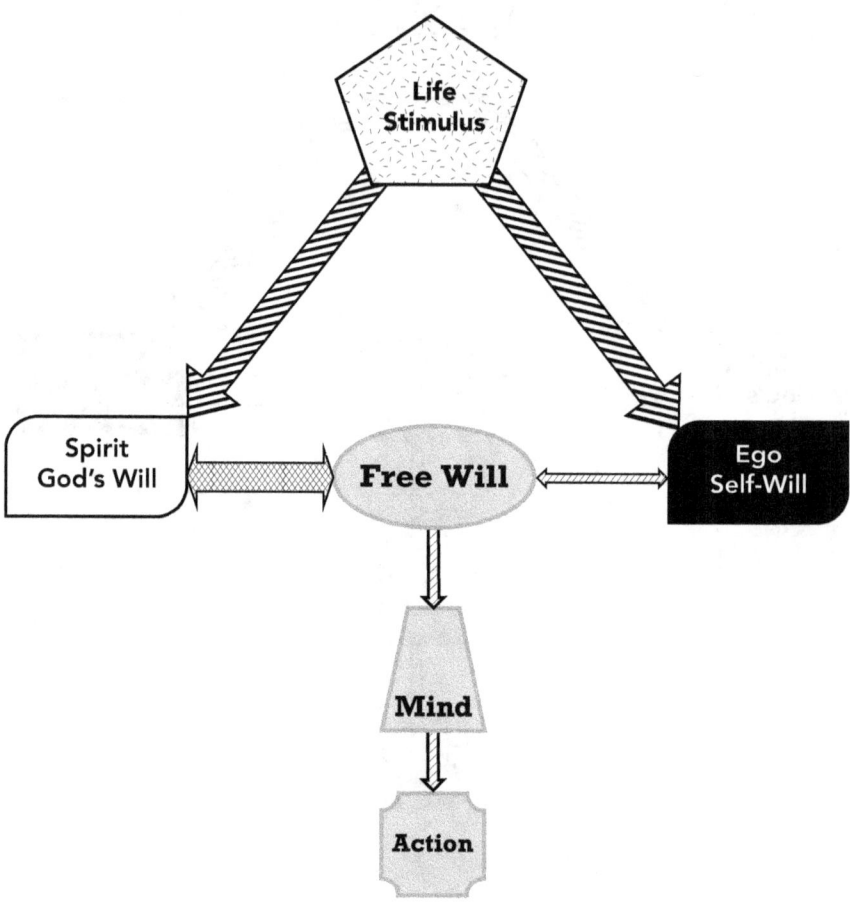

GENESIS

Part 1

The word genesis is defined as "a coming into being." Just like the first book of the Old Testament, where there are two creation stories (Genesis 1:26 to 1:28 and 2:7 to 2:21), I was created twice. The first creation was when I was born. I was born in the Bronx, New York, on July 22, 1949 at 1:00 PM EDT (all you astrologers and numerologist can have fun with this info) into an Orthodox Jewish, middle class family. My father was a taxi driver when I was born. Later he went to work for the New York City Metropolitan Transit Authority (MTA). My mother, as was the way of those times, was a housewife, staying home to look after myself and my younger sister who is eight years my junior.

In order for you to better understand my family dynamics I should share a little bit more with you about my family. Mom was my protector whenever dad was on a rampage. I was always led to believe that I was the reason for these outbursts. The usual explanations I was subjected to were, "I was ruining his life," "I was pissing him off," "He didn't want to hit me or yell at me but I was making him so angry he couldn't control himself." This created problems between mom and dad and eventually led to them sleeping in separate bedrooms; which I, of course, blamed myself for. It never dawned on me as a child that when mom and dad would fight about how to deal with me, that I was not the cause of their arguments, that mom and dad just didn't know how to communicate and work with each other.

My sister was, from the very beginning, the apple of my father's eye. What this did to me was reinforce my own, perceived, inadequacies. What this meant in day-to-day life was that I inflicted my resentments and wrath upon my sister. Didn't I learn how to do that from my father? How come I didn't learn compassion from my own suffering? Why is human history riddled with examples of the abused becoming the abuser even as they are being abused? For example the ongoing history of the Jewish people. Another example is the early Christians abusing Gnostic Christians at the same time they were being persecuted by the Romans.

Some very significant life lessons were instilled in me during these formative years. The first was that I was not okay. How could I be alright if I was responsible for all the problems in the lives of my parents? How could I be alright if, no matter how hard I tried, I could not stop whatever it was I was doing or not doing to anger dad? The second lesson was much more subtle than the first one. If I was responsible for how dad felt, then who was responsible for how I felt? What I learned was to blame whomever was close by and/or whomever was different. You see, dad was full of anger, hate and distrust. I wasn't the only recipient of dad's anger. Anger, like any emotion, expressed frequently enough becomes addictive and like with any addiction the addict develops tolerance so the addict needs more and more and gets less and less from their consumption. Co-workers, people of color, government institutions, bosses at work, etc. were also blamed for dad's lot in life.

A connected lesson I learned was that it was alright to be abusive, especially in the confines of one's own home. Unfortunately, as I grew into a teenager, my anger became so intense, so all consuming, that I was, for the most part, unable to control it. We lived in a neighborhood made up of single family homes and apartment buildings. Dad would always be warm and friendly to our neighbors and was usually available to give them a ride somewhere or to carry their packages for them. This created a recurring dynamic wherein a neighbor would approach me on the street and tell me what a wonderful father I had.

I can't begin to express the pain and self-doubt this caused me to experience, since the dad I knew was angry and abusive more often than not. There had to be something wrong with me to be causing these reactions in dad. This led to another one of those dysfunctional life lessons. I learned it was acceptable behavior to vent one's anger at one's loved ones. I earned a Masters, or maybe even a Doctorate, in this category. Just ask my first and/or second wife. The things I did to them, the abuse I subjected them to should have gotten me arrested, thrown in jail and the key lost forever. Fortunately, God either had other plans for me and/or knew better.

Some of the other lessons I received a Masters or PhD in were that my emotions and my perceptions, along with my thinking and behaviors, were not in sync with the world I lived in and this was not a good thing. Regarding my emotions, there were numerous times as a child when I would express pain, usually by crying, and be told, "Stop crying or I'll give you something to really cry about." The reverse was also true. When I would laugh at something the typical response I received was "What's so funny?" What I came to believe after repeated experiences of having my emotions challenged was that I was out of tune with the rest of the world. This caused me to reinforce the concept within myself that I wasn't constructed for this existence.

Remember the statement "We don't do poisonous quantities of dangerous chemicals because we're happy?" Maybe you're getting a clearer picture as to the unhappiness behind which I became the drug addict I was to become. One more contributing factor should be listed at this juncture.

I will describe my beliefs on karma later. I bring the topic up now to explain the final pin being stuck in the Voodoo doll that was me as a child. I believe that we are all gifted with whatever talents we require in order to fulfill the karma we came into our life to meet ourselves in. For example, we need to meet ourselves as a celebrity to have the opportunity to learn how to define who and what we are. We will enter this existence with the volume turned up as an athlete, for instance. I entered this life with a couple of gifts that I would need to become the spiritual counselor I have become. These gifts, as best as I can describe them, are an increased sense of empathy and an ability to see a much larger, more complete picture than is being presented. How the latter manifested was the gift of recognizing both the cause and the effect in their proper sequence in any given situation.

There were numerous instances when, in early childhood, I would share the perceptions these gifts would provide me with others, only to be told by them that they had no idea what I was talking about. The gift would never go away. Throughout my active addiction I used the gift secretly, never sharing the source of the insights I had. The most prevalent use was to connect with females on a deep level for the sole purpose of getting laid. It wasn't until I got into recovery that I realized, with the help of a friend, that my gift was truly an asset and not a liability. When assets were viewed as liabilities, coupled with the other dysfunctional lessons I embraced, is it any wonder that I became a drug addict? Maybe the wonder is that I survived my original self to become my reborn self? There has been an ongoing debate over nature versus nurture. In hindsight I have come to believe that both are tools of karma. How else can the combination of my experiences and gifts be explained?

In order to provide a more complete picture I should expand upon the family dynamic even further. Mom came from an upper middle class family. My maternal grandfather owned his own business. My maternal aunts and uncle also had upper middle class status. Mom's eldest sister married a doctor. Mom's other sister married a man who owned his own business. Mom's brother owned his own taxi medallion.

Dad came from a lower class family. My paternal grandparents lived in an area of the Bronx that was transforming into a racial ghetto. They never moved from their apartment and were one of the last white families in their neighborhood. Dad's father and mother were Eastern European immigrants. My paternal grandfather was a laborer. Dad originally drove a taxi under someone else's medallion. Dad then got a job working for the MTA in New York City. Dad was a hard worker and rose from a token clerk to a supervisor.

What this background is setting up is the dynamic between dad and my mom's family. Because mom was the youngest sibling, the baby of the family, her sisters and brother never hesitated in imposing their opinions on my mom and dad's life. This imposition, of course, didn't stop with mom and dad, it extended to my sister's and my life as well. And, boy, did they have opinions. In looking back, what made it even more difficult for me was that they had differing opinions of who I should be and what I should be doing. Whenever we went visiting I was able to provide whoever we visited with the image of me that I knew they wanted to see. The problem was when the whole family was together I didn't have a universally acceptable image. Up until the time when I could excuse myself from attending, I made myself as invisible as I could while in attendance. This was usually accomplished by parking myself in front of a television, watching whatever sporting event was being televised, even if I didn't give a damn about it. Think golf.

Another, early, but distorted life lesson that grew out of these family get togethers was that I never learned how to be social during large meal gatherings. Due to the fact that mom was the youngest, by some significant years, of all her siblings, I, age wise, fell into a group of one. My older cousins were years ahead of me and their children were years behind me. I had no one my age to relate to. This, along with the need to get out of the house in my early teens, led me to develop the habit of eating incredibly fast. I probably was swallowing my food half chewed, at best. I, throughout my active addict/non-recovery years, avoided large gatherings as best as I could. Being loaded helped me get through the ones I couldn't avoid. The real terror set in during early recovery, where it was encouraged and expected that I, as a newcomer to a recovery group, would go out for coffee and/or a meal after a meeting. I remember sitting at tables where there were 15 or 20 individuals in attendance. I sat there like I was watching a tennis match. I would look from left to right and back again like I was following the ball. I didn't know if I should say something, wait to be addressed or what. So, for the most part, I sat there in silent discomfort.

Don't read into this that I have become a consummate social animal. I haven't. What I have become is comfortable with who I am and that there isn't anything wrong with me because I don't like to participate in large gatherings. This story has a flip side. I was always comfortable at a meal with no more than two others in attendance. I'm not sure why, it just is.

Getting back to the original thought, this imposing of opinions extended to my life, and later, to my sister's. Mom, dad, sis and I lived with mom's parents in their five-room, two-bedroom, and one-bathroom apartment. This lasted until, when I was 10, my grandmother died and my grandfather moved in with his oldest daughter. It was due to my grandmother's passing that I finally got my own room and a real bed. Up until that time I slept on a cot in the dining room. Sleeping was problematic, because in the dining room was a functioning, metallic grandfathers clock. Not only did it **TICK-TOCK** instead of tick-tock all day and all night long, but it also chimed on the half hour, as well as the hour. The hour chimes were one for each hour and the half-hour chimes were always singular. By itself that would have been no great deal but in my damaged mind it was very significant, for a couple of reasons. The first was that when I finally got a bed and room of my own, I had to sleep in a room and a bed that someone had died in. I was there when she died, I saw it happen, so there was no fudging the facts. Secondly, I lost the companionship of my grandfather, who was an advocate and a real source of comfort. My grandmother I could live without. She was senile for a good number of years and I saw her as the competition for everyone else's attention and love. I used to tease and taunt her and, when my behavior was reported, I used her senility as the source of her delusions and the reason for my innocence. I probably created karma to meet myself in somewhere down the line.

I'm not sure what a normal childhood means and looks like, so I don't want to label mine. I will concede that if I were born 40 or so years later I would probably have had all kinds of alphabet designations, such as ADD or ADHD, alongside my name. Back then I was just a problem child. This is relevant because it created problems for my parents, especially dad. My dad, in retrospect, needed me to be, if not perfect, at least socially acceptable. I wasn't. This frustrated dad to no end. Every time I did something wrong, it was not viewed as a lesson but as blight against the family name. Either due to my alphabet disorders or my basic rebellious nature, I never lived up to what dad expected of me. I wasn't the only one in this family meeting themselves in karma. This brought about an ever increasing abusive response from dad. The response ran the chain from verbal to emotional and to, more often than not, physical. I was constantly being told that I was ruining dad's life, that I was making him angry, that I was pissing him off. No matter how hard I tried, I kept stumbling over myself and disappointing dad. At some point during my formative years, I was given the definitive explanation of why I was the way I was. Dad informed me one day, in a fit of anger over what I do not remember, that the best part on me had run down his leg. I want you to understand, that I was so young at the time that I didn't comprehend the sexual reference made in that statement. What I did understand was that I wasn't whole and that the best part of me was missing.

As bad as the above was, I believe what did my psyche even more damage were the times when I did something wrong and dad would punish me by ignoring me. One moment we could be the best of buddies and the next I didn't exist. I could talk, cry, or plead to no avail. Dad wouldn't even look my way. My memory may be a little faulty here, but I believe this place of non-existence, at times, lasted for days, not just hours. The pain of non-existence was so much greater than the physical and emotional pains I experienced from the other abuses. I believe the long term scars created by this abandonment was one of the main reasons for the conflicts in my second marriage.

When I could no longer live with the image I had of myself and the lighter addictions I practiced, such as sleeping, candy, comic books and music, stopped working, I took the necessary steps to escape me. I call them lighter addictions because they met the qualifying conditions of obsession and compulsion without having the self-destructive properties of drug addiction. I was always thinking about them, especially the candy and the comic books. I would steal money from mom's purse to feed these habits. While I was doing this I believed mom was obtuse and never knew how much money she had. Looking back, with an eye of wisdom, I now believe she knew what I was doing but didn't say anything in order to protect me from dad's wrath.

I started drinking during my 12th year of life. My first drink, outside of the Passover wine, was the scotch my father bought for my upcoming Bar Mitzvah. There was a case of Ballantine Scotch in the closet in my room. I don't remember what precipitated my need to so desperately escape reality but I do remember that I drank a whole bottle. My head spun one way, the room spun the other way and then I passed out. When I came to I had puked all over myself, my head felt like it was being constantly hit with something and I couldn't wait to do it again.

And do it again I did, and more. I quickly graduated to drugs. They were readily available and so was I. I wasn't choosey, I did as much as I could of whatever I could get my hands on. This led to a 26-year drug (yes, alcohol is a drug) addiction problem. I believe that one of the side effects of doing all those drugs for all those years is that I am chronologically challenged. I'm not sure of the exact years and dates when some of the events occurred that I am about share with you, but they did occur and the timing isn't as important as what took place.

You may ask, "Why did I turn to alcohol to escape?" The answer is, surprise, dad. I'm not sure of my exact age, somewhere around maybe 10 or 11 years old, when I was deemed old enough to accompany mom and dad to nighttime family gatherings. What I experienced there set the tone for my soon to come drug addictive behaviors. Specifically, I saw a different dad. He was warm, friendly and, above all else, happy. As the gathering progressed dad became warmer, friendlier and happier. What dawned on me was that this transformation of dad was fueled by the glass of amber liquid he was constantly drinking from. What I came to find out was that the amber liquid was scotch. So when that need, at 12 years old, came over me to escape, of course

I turned to scotch. If it could change dad so radically, I had no doubt it would do the same for me.

In retrospect I should have known something was out of sync between my body and my head's desire to do, what became, poisonous quantities of dangerous chemicals. Just like my first experience with alcohol was truly a sign not to trespass, so was my first experience with drugs. The first drug I tried was marijuana. The first time I smoked it nothing happened. Why did I go back for more? Maybe, because I was desperate to escape? Maybe, because I was so codependent that I wanted all the guys and girls who I hung on the corner with to think I was cool and to like me? Probably both of the above and other factors not considered. So, I went back for more and experienced intense paranoia. Again, this did not deter me.

I had similar warning indicators the first time I used other drugs. The first time I used amphetamines I stayed awake tweaking, listening to Alison Steele, The Night Bird. Her show ended at 2 AM and I was no closer to sleeping than I was when her show first started at 10 PM. My best thinking at the time was maybe if I masturbated, I would be able to sleep. Unusual thinking for a 13-year-old male? I think not. That's when I really freaked out. My penis had shriveled up and nothing, and I mean nothing, I could do brought it back to life. I was terrified. Did that stop me from doing some more? Hell, no. I just was a little more cautious when I was doing them. If there was a chance of sexual activity I refrained from their consumption.

The first time I used cocaine I thought my heart was going to explode through my chest. It didn't and I continued to use cocaine knowing I would have some discomfort but I would survive it. Escaping myself was more important than suffering some discomfort.

Narcotics Anonymous, a Twelve Step Fellowship, usually opens its meetings with a series of readings. One of them is "How It Works?." There is a line in that reading that states "We didn't become addicted in one day, so remember - easy does it." That statement doesn't ring true to me. If I weren't addicted in one day, if I weren't predisposed (karma?) why would I have returned to using drugs that created such a negative first experience?

Part 2

What I consider my real genesis occurred in the summer of 1979. I consider this my real genesis because for the first time in my 30 years of existence I actually gave thought to the concept that there was something going on that was not explainable by any known science that I had knowledge of. I wasn't yet ready to embrace the concept of God. There were too many negative associations for that to happen. Being born Jewish had turned me completely off to the concept of God. To me God and religion were synonymous, and everything I had experienced with religion left an awful taste in my mouth. It starts with having the knowledge that, throughout history people were killed for being Jewish. I was repeatedly reminded that six million Jews were killed during the recently ended World War II. What kind of God allows Its chosen people to be killed just for worshiping It? If that weren't enough, there was also all the times that my father would return from Saturday worship services and continue to be the same angry, abusive individual that he was before he left for the services. Add in a great deal of perceived hypocrisy and episodes of blackmailing me to attend services, my association of God and religion, and my distaste for it should be clear. My basic response to anyone who tried to engage me in a conversation about God was that I would not share my drugs and they would not share their God and we might be able to get along.

Anyway, back to genesis. I went on a vacation to Club Med in Martinique. Back then, Martinique was the wild party club, not the family club the other locations promoted. Upon arriving at the club I dropped my belongings in my room and went out to explore the area and search out a companion for at least the rest of the day. As soon as I began my scouting mission I was approached by a woman, not without attractions, about my age who offered to do my numbers for me. Not knowing better I thought I was being offered some form of exotic, kinky sex. Boy, was I going to enjoy this place!

I don't remember her name, I may have never been given it. She guided me to a grove of trees at the perimeter of the club. Wow, we were going to do this outdoors. This place just kept getting better and better. She asked me to spell my name and what my birthday was. I thought these questions rather strange considering the direction I believed this encounter was headed in but who was I to create waves. What followed opened up a world for me that I never knew existed. She proceeded to tell me my life story, my conflicts with my father, about my recently ended first marriage and other information that was not only "dead nuts on" but beyond anything she could have surmised about me in our short time together. I'm not sure how long this session lasted, time was not a factor. I do remember her finishing her reading, getting up and walking back towards the compound. I sat there alone, stunned (I'm not sure for how long), blown away by the experience and trying to make some sense of it.

I finally decided I had a bunch of questions to ask her, the foremost was what had just happened and how did she do it. I headed back to the compound in search of her. And search I did. I searched and searched to no avail. Everyone I asked about her did not know her. I mean I really searched. I was able to describe her in detail to everyone, but no one knew of her. I inquired of the club staff if any guests had recently departed and was informed that had not happened. For the next day I continued to look for her, getting no closer to finding her than I had previously.

Looking back, with the understandings I currently believe, I am sure that this was an Angel sent to get my attention and she sure did. If an Angel in the form of a male had been sent, I would never have engaged and would have not received the lesson I needed to have. God knew who I was and what it would take to get my attention. In retrospect I firmly believe this was an intervention designed to return me to the path of my karmic blueprint. It did, it just was not instantaneous.

Returning to the path is not an event nor a destination, it is a journey that lasts more than a lifetime. I returned home from Martinique on a Sunday to find a pile of mail waiting for me. What

I can see in retrospect is that Divine Presence had the next experience waiting for me. You see, I didn't just separate out the bills from the junk and discard the junk like I always did. I looked at each piece of mail including an adult education course catalog from the local community college. What I found was an introductory course to astrology. I was drawn to the course. I was looking for some understanding behind the experience I had in Martinique. I called the college first thing Monday morning to see if I could enroll. I was informed that I had called just in time as there was only one slot left.

I don't recall much but I do remember the instructor's opening statement. What she said was that astrology is about possibilities not unalterable destinations. She went on to say that free will rules all and we all have free will.

I learned a lot about the mechanics of astrology and by the end of the course I was able to create a chart and interpret it. At the end of the semester the instructor told us that she would be teaching an intermediate course the following semester. I waited anxiously for the catalog to arrive. When it did I searched for but couldn't find the class listed. The introductory class wasn't listed either. I called the college and was informed that the previous semester's course was a trial run and the decision had been made not to continue with the course.

Was the astrology course as a follow up to my numerology experience a coincidence or a random occurrence? I believe not. You, the reader, are free to believe whatever you choose.

KARMA IS

Why am I including this subject at this juncture? The reason is simple. I am here to serve. If you, the reader, do not read any further than this most basic thesis on our relationship with God, then the time and energy you have expended will not have gone for naught. Neither will have mine. You see it took me the greater part of 60 years to gather these understandings. Life would have been so much more serene and fulfilling if someone would have presented me with this information during my childhood. That, however, was not my karma. Instead I was given myths, parables and metaphors that were lumped together under the title "Judaism" and was instructed to blindly remember and obey that which was interpreted for me by those who were more learned.

Before I go on any further I feel I should, at this point, share with you my belief of karma. Karma is manifested in three different aspects of our lives. In order of our human experience, there is day-to-day karma, life-to-life karma and group karma. Karma is cause and effect, not punishment and reward. Karma is a reactive force at the very core of all that exists in this plane of existence.

From ancient Shamanism we learn that there are two realities: ordinary and non-ordinary. Shamanism goes on further to explain that part of our Soul occupies our body in ordinary reality, and part of our Soul resides in the spirit realm, non-ordinary reality. The part that resides in the spirit realm is aware of our karmic blueprint and communicates to the part in the physical realm, guiding it, while allowing for free will, to best keep the Soul on its path. Because the guiding Soul is in the spirit realm it can and does communicate in enacting plans with other guiding Souls to best facilitate the path of all the participating Souls to keep every Soul as close as possible to its blueprint.

The feelings that the physical body experiences are inconsequential. It is the sensations that the Soul experiences that teach the Soul. The body is the teaching vehicle but it is temporary. Therefore, what the body feels will only last for, at most, the remainder of its lifetime. What the Soul feels lasts for eternity. Those lessons create, based on the intensity of the experience, day-to-day karma as well as, if warranted, life-to-life karma.

The purpose of this elaborate mechanism is to teach the Soul. The Earth plane of existence is the only one a Soul will reside in that allows the Soul to feel the ramifications of the thoughts, emotions and actions that free will chooses to participate in. If free will's choice is to act out in self-will, it creates pain for not only the Earth Soul but the Spirit Soul as well. Create enough pain and the Earth Soul withdraws to the spirit realm. This creates the need for what we call the Shamanic journey. Acting out in accordance with God's will creates equanimity and both Souls experience the joy of oneness.

The following are my definitions of the three types of karma.

Day-To-Day Karma

In day-to-day Karma, the Karmic Forces react to what we do, think, feel (especially fear) and/or believe on a regular and consistent basis, and makes it manifest in our life. It gives us an opportunity to meet ourselves and decide if we will manifest God's will or self-will in that aspect of our existence. In its most simplistic terms we get to decide if we want to live in faith or live in fear. If we choose faith we then have to demonstrate it. If we choose fear then we will be placed at another crossroads that will give us the opportunity to choose again.

Karma is also created anytime we place any aspect of the material existence ahead of our spiritual existence. As Jesus is quoted as teaching (the Gospel According to Saint Mark, the *King James Version*, Chapter 10, Verses 23 - 25):

> "And Jesus looked round about, and saith unto his disciples, how hardly shall they that have riches enter into the kingdom of God! And the disciples were astonished at his words. But Jesus answereth again, and saith unto them, Children, how hard is it for them that trust in riches to enter into the kingdom of God! It is easier for a camel to go through the eye of a needle, than for a rich man to enter into the kingdom of God."

My interpretation of Jesus' teaching is that in those ancient of times large cities were walled for defense from marauders. During daylight hours there was a large, defended gate that several humans and animals could pass through at one time. During night hours the large gate was closed and barred. Built within the large gate was a human size gateway. This was the eye of the needle. In order for a traveler and their camel to enter the city the traveler would have to unload the camel, coax the camel to its knees and guide the camel to crawl through the gate. Once inside the city the camel would then have to be reloaded in order to transport the merchandise to the traveler's ultimate destination within the city. As strenuous and tedious as this was it was easier, according to Jesus, than getting a rich man into the Kingdom of God. Why? Because the rich man, was attached to his riches and instead of surrendering to Spirit and doing its good works he was accumulating his wealth, sacrificing service to others, and worshiping to and believing that the material wealth would somehow make him a better individual.

Life-To-Life Karma

Life-to-life karma is the one we bring with us from one lifetime to the next. In order for this to come to pass the Law of Reincarnation was established. Reincarnation is the vehicle karma utilizes to fulfill its

Law. We enlist the aid of other Souls who are with us in our Collective to create situations in the flesh that will afford us the opportunity to meet ourselves in a way that provides us with the ability to satisfy some of our karmic debt. Of course, this is a two way street. We are, at the same time, affording our Soul mates the same opportunity they are affording us. The term Collective refers to a community of Souls each and every one of us belong to. The Collectives vary in size from a few hundred Souls to a few billion Souls. In all, there are one hundred forty four thousand Collectives. (The Revelation of Saint John the Divine, the *King James Version*, Chapter 7, Verse 4) reads as follows:

> "And I heard the number of them which were
> sealed: and there were sealed a hundred
> and forty and four thousand of all the tribes
> of the children of Israel."

I believe what Saint John the Divine is referring to in this passage are the Soul Collectives. The message Saint John is being given is that the Law of Karma and all the related Laws will not pass from existence until every Soul in every Collective has achieved reunification with God.

The only karma we incur is our own. We can reincarnate infinitely with the same Souls; however, it is only a good working relationship and not obligation that will have us returning over and over again with the same Souls. This collective within a collective is known as a Soul group. One significant importance of this karma is that it forms the basis of spiritual forgiveness. How can we not forgive both ourselves and others for the perceived harm done to us when we have a belief that what we experienced was done at our behest. We are no longer victims, we are volunteers.

One of the misunderstandings that accompanies life-to-life karma is the recognition process God utilizes to connect us with our helping Soul mates when we are in the flesh. That immediate, out of nowhere, powerful, energetic attraction we experience while going about our day-to-day business is God's way of facilitating our recognizing and connecting to our helping Souls. All too often this is misinterpreted as love or lust or some other form of physical attraction that must be explored. While sometimes it is that, most of the time it is only a sign that we have met a teacher whom we are here to also teach. We, as a culture, in our desperate need to find love outside of ourselves, have distorted the concept of a Soul mate. We believe it is a happily ever after, 'til death do us part,' validation of our existence. In God's world Soul mates are the bearers of our most important lessons. The more we can grasp and implement this into our perceptions, the easier our human lives will become and the quicker we will grow in spirit and we will reap the added bonus of not creating new karma.

The following was sent to me years ago without any identification of the author. I believe it describes, beautifully, the point I am trying to make. I named the piece "Reason, Season and Lifetime." It reads as follows:

> "People come into your life for a Reason, a Season or a Lifetime. When you know which one it is, you will know what to do for that person. When someone is in your life for a Reason, it is usually to meet a need you have expressed. They have come to assist you through a difficulty, to provide you with guidance and support, to aid you physically, emotionally or spiritually. They may seem like a godsend and they are. They are there for the Reason you need them to be. Then, without any wrongdoing on your part or at a convenient time, this person will say or do something to bring the relationship to an end. Sometimes they die. Sometimes they walk away. Sometimes they act up and force you to take a stand. What we must realize is that our need has been met, our desire fulfilled, their work is done. The prayer you sent up has been answered and now it is time to move on.
>
> "Some people come into your life for a Season, because your turn has come to share, grow or learn. They bring you an experience of peace or make you laugh. They may teach you something you have never done. They

usually give you an unbelievable amount of joy. Believe it, it is real. But only for a Season!

"Lifetime relationships teach you Lifetime lessons, things you must build upon in order to have a solid emotional foundation. Your job is to accept the lesson, love the person and put what you have learned to use in all other relationships and areas of your life. It is said that love is blind but friendship is clairvoyant."

Group Karma

Group karma is the merging of both life-to-life and day-to-day karma coming together in a human collective. The human collective can take on many different forms, from gender to race to religion to nationality to family/clan groupings.

GRACE IS

Day-to-day karma is the most important karma we work with. It has the power to create our own reality. It also has the power to pay back lifetime karma at an accelerated rate. This is known as the Law of Grace. The following are some Edgar Cayce psychic readings in which, in their entirety, are Cayce's explanation of this Law.

Reading 2981-1, Paragraphs 5, 6 & 7:

"Hence those experiences which have brought distortions in the material plane are not merely because of karmic law, but the application of karmic law in the life of the individual entity. Thus we find those greater opportunities for the entity meeting same, not only in the law of cause and effect - or karma – but also in the application of the Law of Grace. The activities of the entity, thusly, are tied in the material, in the mental, in the spiritual, with what the entity does about the choices made."

Reading 99-8, Paragraph 7:

"He that gives a cup of water in HIS name loses not HIS reward" - not as pay, not as recompense, but SERVICE is asked of all men, rather than sacrifice. In sacrifice there is penance, but grace doth more greatly abound to him who sheds the love of the Father upon those that the body may contact from day-to-day."

Reading 262-2, Question 5:

"Practice makes perfect; and as one practices, puts in use, in word, in deed, day by day, so does one grow in grace, in knowledge, in understanding; and He that would be the greatest among you, let him be the servant of all."

There exists in the physical realm the concept of Grace. The concept of Grace is different but similar to the Law of Grace. It is this realm's version of the greater application. What Grace means is unmerited reward. Because our society, our culture, is contaminated by the misconception of a punishing God we have come to believe that Grace must be earned. That is false. **GOD IS** Unconditionally Loving. Therefore, Grace is our birthright. We do not, I repeat, we DO NOT have to earn Grace, we have to stop blocking it. Every time we act out of self-will, we add to a personal shield that blocks Grace. The more energy we give to self-will guided acts the stronger we make that shield and the more Grace we block. The more energy we give to God's guidance, the more porous our shield becomes and the more Grace enters.

There is one other Law that is relevant here. It is the Law of Free Will. As explained earlier, the Law of Free Will allows us, as Spiritual Human beings to choose. We get to choose, infinite times during the course of a day, between God's Will and self-will.

The catch is that as Spiritual Human beings we are incapable of knowing what percentage of each of the three Laws are in action during any given situation. If we cannot determine the influences we are under in any given situation and **GOD IS** unconditionally loving, then that knowledge must not be of any value. If that knowledge is of no value, then what really matters? What really matters is what we do and the motivations for those actions! If our actions are selfless, we will be exercising Free Will, not creating karma and moving towards the Law of Grace.

I WAS

There is a gap in this narrative that needs to be filled in – the time between my first drink in 1961 and my experience in Martinique, in 1979. I'm not here to convince you how bad I was or to have you think that I think there is something glamorous to what I did. I'm not and there isn't. I want to look at it from the perspective that The First Cause, bidden or unbidden, is always present (thank you Fr. Murphy for that amazing concept). Let me get as clear as I can here. I did everything I could to obliterate my life and wreaked havoc and toxicity on anyone who was unfortunate enough to cross my path. When I celebrate my recovery birthday at a meeting I state two perceptions. The first is that I didn't accumulate years, I accumulated days, hours and minutes because recovery, like life, is one moment at a time. The other is that I stand to show others what is possible. I seek no applause. I'm like the arsonist who burned down his own house and managed to escape with only singes on his ass. The glory, the applause belongs to the Divine Presence not me.

As I stated earlier I disconnected from the concept of God early on. The only reason I am here to tell this tale is because of an unconditionally loving Deity. A lot of what is to follow are realizations that I came to believe in working my Second Step, "We came to believe that a Power greater than ourselves could restore us to sanity," with my first sponsor. You see, I didn't come to recovery beaming with God, spirit or anything that might be construed as falling into that category. So coming to believe that there was a Power greater than myself was a big challenge. The most important question on my Second Step read

"Has there ever been a time that, in spite of your best thinking, feeling and action, the consequences were not as near as severe as they could or should have been?" my first response was "Huh?"

The first question was "How many times did I drive under the influence?" My response was, "More times than I could possibly count."

The next question was "How many people did I kill while driving under the influence?" My answer was "None." My sponsor's response to my answer was, "Could I come to believe that a Power greater than myself was looking out for me during all those times?" My answer was "No." You see, back in the days, part of my coping mechanisms for the behaviors I was practicing was the denial concept that I drove better under the influence than I did when I was straight, though I'm not sure I ever drove straight. There were a number of things that I never experienced not being under the influence until I entered recovery, driving wasn't the only thing. Sex was another, but we'll deal with that in another chapter.

The question and answer exchange went on for quite a while. After each Q & A my sponsor repeated the question about coming to believe and I repeated the answer, with a little less conviction, "no."

The questions, usually following my sponsor's sharing of his story were:

"How many accidents did you have?" "1½" (You see back then, in the state of New York, there was a no fault law that split the fault evenly if the damages were under a certain threshold).

"How many DUIs did I get?" "None."

"How many near misses were there?" Again, there were too many to recount, but two instances jumped into my mind. The first one was driving with Mo in his new, I believe, 61 Impala, on the Sprain Brook Parkway in Westchester, New York. Mo, like most of my friends of that period was a user. Mo, under the influence, punched the gas and the car spun out of control and started heading down the road sideways. I don't know how far we went sideways but we didn't encounter any other cars in our skid. Then, for no reason connected with anything Mo did, the car straightened itself out and Mo was able to regain control.

The other near miss occurred when I was returning from a friend's house in northern New Jersey via the lower level of the George Washington Bridge. Do I need to remind you I was loaded at the time? I was slightly behind and to the right of a soda truck. Back in those days there were still individuals who delivered soda and seltzer to your door. Their trucks were open behind the cab and the cases of soda/seltzer were in slots along the side of the truck and balanced on top of one another at the crest of the truck.

I was driving along jamming out to the radio when this force of a voice resonated throughout my entire being, ordering me to "floor it, immediately." I didn't have a choice to not respond, the voice was so powerful, the instruction so urgent. I floored the gas and was past the soda truck in an instant. Just as I was alongside the cab of the truck I heard a loud crash. Looking in my rear view mirror I saw a couple of cases of soda had fallen off the truck landing in the space I had just occupied.

This brought up other episodes that, in their recall, were weakening my resolve that a Power greater than myself didn't exist. I will list a few more to show the extent of God's intervention in my life and the level of stubbornness and denial that was in my life at that time.

The first was an encounter in Poe Park, in the Bronx, New York, where about a dozen or so of my buddies and I encountered a larger group of younger guys who claimed they were the junior chapter of the gang called the Ducky Boys. As we chased them out of the park they threatened us that they were going to go get their older members and come back and kick our asses. We decided that a few of us should go get help while the rest of us remained behind and held claim to our turf. In an act of insanity I volunteered to stay behind. The outcome was that neither the Ducky Boys nor our friends with reinforcements returned. Our friends went to the local bar and wound up staying and getting drunk. In spite of my best thinking, feeling and actions I survived.

There was an episode at the Synagogue that I was forced to attend, where, during a bazaar, I, under the influence got into a fight with a drunk cop who was there as security. It all started because, during those years, day or night, I always wore dark gray sunglasses. As soon as the officer saw me he approached me and ordered me to remove my sunglasses. Having no use or respect for authority (thanks dad) I refused. The officer attempted to remove the glasses and I shoved him away from me. He attacked me and I fought back. His drunkenness gave me the advantage. Before either one of us could inflict much, if any, damage on the other the senior members of the congregation intervened and because they knew my father and probably because the officer was Irish, they threatened to report the officer for being drunk if he tried to arrest me. He agreed and while I was being escorted out I was advised, in no uncertain terms, not to return. In spite of my best thinking, feeling and actions I didn't wind up beaten, shot or incarcerated.

Another example of God's Grace occurred at the premature end of a Smokey Robinson & The Miracles concert at the Schaefer Circle (it might have been named after another beer manufacturer at the time) in Central Park in Manhattan. I had gone to the concert with a few of my friends. I was loaded. Hell, I never went anywhere not loaded.

Maybe I should take a moment here to define loaded. To me being loaded was being in a state where I was not feeling the ramifications of being Phil. I was feeling no pain and I would do whatever I had to do to sustain that state. Coming down was not an option. Being loaded does not imply the use of any one substance. I was a garbage head. I would use anything and everything that was available. I never was loyal to any one substance or any one person, place or thing. Not being me was the most important thing, not what drug I was using. There were times I would use drugs to induce what I would imagine would be an appropriate demonstration or response for an occasion. A good example would be that I never did anything that would induce the nod if I was going to a party or a dance club. One of the great all time combinations was disco and cocaine. Conversely, if I thought I should be somber, I chased the nod. Being an addict was a full time endeavor and encompassed more than drugs. I used anything and everything that helped me avoid acknowledging who and what I perceived I was. I used sex, food, gambling, and even sleep as avoidance behaviors, just to name a few.

Returning to the narrative, the concert had just begun when a group of individuals from the audience jumped on stage and started dancing to the music. This annoyed Smokey and he requested that they get off the stage. They didn't, nor was there any security to enforce Smokey's wishes, so Smokey and the Miracles left the stage. Everyone waited for them to return but they didn't. This triggered a riot, with attendees in the mezzanine throwing things, such as metal milk crates, down on the exiting crowd. Understand that the vast majority of attendees were black, with us white folk making up a very insignificant minority. The anger spilled out of Central Park to the surrounding areas with violence and looting being the main activities. I believe only Divine Intervention was responsible for the small group of us white folk wandering around trying to find our vehicle (nobody seemed to remember where we parked it) in a sea of black anger and destruction without being attacked.

Having survived one very close encounter with a race riot should be enough for any one life. Whatever the lesson, I needed to experience it twice. My friend Ricky and I decided to spend a weekend at Asbury Park, New Jersey. The prime motivation was to pick up and party with some Jersey Girls, long before Bruce Springsteen made them famous. We arrived by bus and when it came time to leave we departed the same way. When we arrived back in New York City at the bus terminal there were TV cameras and reporters wanting to interview us. As it turned out, Ricky and I got the last bus out of Asbury Park. The riot had begun before we left but just hadn't advanced to the bus terminal, at the time. It was probably a window of five minutes that was the difference between getting out of town and being caught in the riot. We told the reporters that we had a fun time and that we didn't see anything that indicated the underlying tensions that triggered the riot. Fortunately, by God's Grace, that was my last encounter with a riot.

There is one more episode that needs to be recounted here in order to give you a deeper, more thorough understanding of the insanity I practiced as a drug addict and the unbelievable, incomprehensible power of an unconditionally loving Creator. The first episode actually replicated itself. As was my nature, being home for any period of time, either when living with my parents or with my first wife, was something that I couldn't tolerate. I associated home with pain and being outside the home as freedom. I also believed that being home meant that I was missing out on something I would regret. That was not the case 99.5% of the time, but I felt I was disadvantaged enough as I was and that I needed to make myself available at all times as compensation. Anyway, I would hook up with a friend who had a car and we would go park on some dark, lightly trafficked back street in a residential neighborhood or under an overpass on the frontage road of the Major Deegan Expressway. The two incidents I am about to relate took place once in each of the two scenarios described above. Each time my using buddy and I were loaded, drugs and paraphernalia were all over the dashboard and front seat of the car when we saw the reflection of a light directly behind us, in the rear view mirror. The feeling that comes over an individual is something to the effect of "Oh shit, we're busted, jail here we come." By God's unwavering Grace, in each episode, just as the officer arrived at the driver's side window we heard his squawk box go off and he went rushing away, sirens blazing, to some more important event.

One last story. I was driving through one of the old neighborhoods in the south Bronx. The south Bronx was divided up into two ghettos. One was black and the other was mixed Hispanic. The streets were very narrow. They dated back to the horse and buggy days. There were cars parked on either side of the street and it was a challenge to drive down the street without taking off a side view mirror. I, as I always was, was loaded. If memory serves me, my buddy wasn't. Out of nowhere came, from between two parked cars, a ball and a child chasing the ball. I mean the child was right in front of us. The car stopped. Now my buddy was a good driver, but he wasn't that good. I believe God stopped the car not only to save the child but my buddy and myself as well. You see, if we would have run the child over, being two white boys, the police wouldn't have been called. We would have been torn to pieces, and the Sanitation Department would have been called and asked to come clean the blood and the white trash off the street.

Over the course of my spiritual journey, read that as my life, I have come to believe that there are no such things as random occurrences, coincidence, luck or miracles. These are just words human beings have created as a means to describe the events happening in their lives without attributing them to "A Power Greater Than Ourselves." "A Power Greater Than Ourselves" translates into something that is capable of doing things beyond our ability to comprehend. This belief started for me and is firmly rooted in the work I did on the Second Step. I will borrow the legal term "preponderance of evidence" to explain the start of my conversion from an atheist to an individual who believes, as Yogi Bhajan, the since passed over head of North American Sikhdom, used to teach, "if you don't see God in all, you don't see God at all."

This appears as good a place as any to talk about blackouts. The most common form of a blackout that is not organic in nature is probably the one brought about by the severe overuse of drugs. Blackouts can also come about because of other factors but those factors are not why I am here or what I want to discuss. What I want to share with you is what happens in a blackout. Remember a while back I discussed the Shamanic teachings of two realities and how the Soul reacts to pain from the physical body? Well, let's take this a bit deeper. There is a dimension created in the overlap of ordinary and non-ordinary reality. This overlap allows Souls to transition out of the physical realm to the Spirit realm. Christianity calls this dimension purgatory. In most cases the Soul moves on as a natural action. There are, however, instances where Souls either cannot accept their transitional death or are extremely attached to the physical plane. When this happens the Soul hangs out in this overlap dimension. Since the Soul has self-determination and there is no time in this way station, or in the Spirit realm for that matter, by human standards the Soul can remain there for an extended period of time. When self-will creates the conditions that cause a Soul to leave the body one of these disenfranchised Souls enters that body and utilizes it as its own. This is why I could not remember how I started out in the Bronx on Friday and it's now Sunday and I am in Philadelphia, or who this person is in the bed along side of me, or how come my car is parked with the front half of the vehicle on the sidewalk. Ultimately the Soul always returns to the body it has entered this plane in, but it will have no memory of the events the body has partaken of. There have been psychics who claim they can sense crowds of disenfranchised entities in bars. Where better to find a vacated body then the location probably most utilized to self-inflict pain?

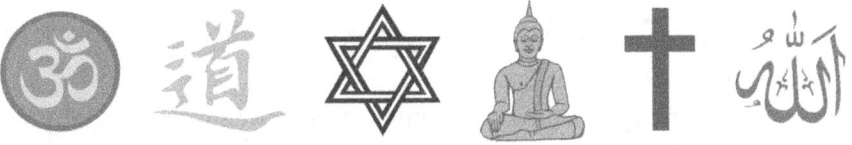

SANCTUARY WAS

Since we are talking about Souls hanging out this is as good a time as any to describe what I did to survive, besides getting loaded, during my teen years. For a significant part of my adolescence my father would work the overnight shift. This was probably due to two factors. The first was dad was constantly going for and achieving higher positions within the MTA. Each promotion started dad at the bottom of the seniority list and obligated him to work the least desirable shift, the overnight. I also believe he chose to keep these shifts, longer than necessary, to avoid life at home. He would come home early morning, go sleep for six to eight hours, get up to take mom shopping or on some other errand (mom didn't drive), come back home, sleep some more, get up for dinner and then start getting ready to leave for work. As far as I was concerned the more time I spent in the house, the greater the chance I would do something to piss dad off. So I ate quickly and left.

I didn't care if I hung out on the corner by myself, sitting on a curb with my back against a lamp pole smoking a joint and/or swallowing some pills. I was free and I was safe. During inclement weather I would go hang out in the Strong Street garage. Strong Street was a one-block-long street that connected University Avenue and Reservoir Avenue. For whatever reason, maybe because of the garage which was situated in the middle of the block and contained a pay phone, and a soda machine which was never closed, the street was the hangout for all the teens in the neighborhood, regardless of age. It was not unusual to have maybe 75 or 100 of us hanging out up and down the block on any given evening.

During daytime hours I would find escape by walking around the 2½ mile circumference of the reservoir that was situated in the neighborhood. The reservoir was something like a fifth level storage backup water supply. I loved the solitude of walking around it. The colder, nastier the weather was, the more desolate the journey was; therefore, the more satisfying it was. I would bundle up in a pea coat my father gave me and walk for what seemed forever. Actually, the pea coat belonged to a sailor whose name was stenciled on the inside. My father was army not navy. Dad claimed he won the pea coat in a craps game. The coat might have been the most precious gift he ever gave me.

As I look back on that time of my life I recognize that the sanctuary that had the greatest impact on me was my friend Rich's family apartment. Rich was one of my childhood buddies who lived in the apartment building diagonally across the street from me. In the context of street football, two-on-two or three-on-three, Rich was always my number one receiver. In sewer stick-ball Rich was always the infielder to my outfielder. We were tight, Rich was the brother I never had.

In retrospect, I believe Rich's parents had a pretty good idea what my life at home was like. Some of that understanding might be attributable to Rich providing information but I believe that it mostly was due to their ability, especially Rich's mom Muriel, of seeing the depth of pain in my eyes. There were more times than I could count where I would walk over to Rich's place to see if he was home. Usually Muriel would answer the door and invite me in whether Rich was home or not. If Rich was not home Muriel would invite me in to watch TV with her and Rich's father Charlie, or to just join her in the kitchen for a drink, non-alcoholic of course, and some conversation. I believe, without a doubt, that these acts of compassion saved what little sanity I possessed and probably kept me from harming myself and/or others. Muriel and Charlie were, without a doubt, the only loving, functional couple I ever observed during the years I spent growing up in the Bronx.

When Lin and I got married in 1996 Rich had already passed over (more on this soon). We were legally married in Elkton, Maryland and held our wedding celebration in Newtown, Pennsylvania. It was a blessing to have been able to reach out to Muriel and Charlie and invite them to the reception and have them both attend. They were the parents I wished I could have had, and I hope they saw the joy and happiness in my eyes. They have since passed over but they will always remain, with gratitude, in my heart.

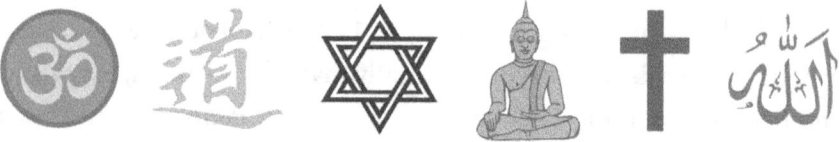

RICH WAS

Let me start by saying I am grateful beyond expression for the karma that brought Rich and me together. The story that preceded this one only covers the start of our relationship, not the full extent of it. I'm going to jump around chronologically and contextually here in order to convey the impact that Rich had on my life.

Rich was diagnosed in his early teens with Gardner's Syndrome (GS). Having GS meant that one's body would create growths, such as polyps, internally. The best thinking of the doctors treating him at that time was that he would not survive his teens. He actually lived to the age of 46. He might have lived even longer if he wasn't so obsessed with proving he was healthy and didn't put so much stress on his body in the quest to prove that.

Rich spent a significant portion of his life drifting in and out of health. He actually made a lot of money being sick. Back in those days an individual could have multiple health insurance policies. Rich had a policy of his own and he was also covered on a separate policy purchased for him by his father. So every time he had a procedure, which was frequently and was expensive, he submitted two claims. Since each policy paid 80%, Rich cleared 60% for himself. After a few decades of doing this Rich accumulated a nice nest egg for himself. There came a time when Rich decided to purchase, as an investment, three 900 phone numbers. Rich came to me and basically told me that he didn't know what to do with these numbers but was confident I was creative enough to come up with a profitable use for them. My first idea, phone sex, was prohibited by the seller. You see, even though

Rich owned the lines he was obligated, contractually, to use the seller's services, such as marketing, advertising operators and accountants.

The idea that next came to me was to run three different trivia lines with a weekly drawing from all the individuals who successfully answered the trivia question for a monetary prize. We were going to have a sports trivia line, a song lyric line and a current events line. We had visions of sugar plum fairies dancing in our heads. We were going to make so much money we wouldn't be able to spend it all. We decided that we didn't have to be in New York City to run this venture. We could do it from anywhere there was a telephone. This led us to the idea of buying a van and outfitting it to accommodate the two of us on a "round the world" voyage. We were going to drive across the United States, head north through Canada to Alaska, cross the Behring Strait by ferry, head south through Russia to China, head west through Asia, tour Africa and then Europe. The journey would end in England where we would sell the van and fly back to New York City. Unfortunately, Rich took ill and this grand plan never materialized.

Why am I telling you this story? Because, there came a time in my life where my second marriage imploded at the same time my employment terminated. Being clean, but not really in recovery at the time, I decided to hit the road–not quite as ambitiously as the journey Rich and I had planned, just a jaunt around the U.S. So I called Rich and asked him if he wanted to join me on this venture. Rich was willing, but by the time I settled my affairs and bought and outfitted a van it was coming up on winter. We decided I was going to head to Florida for the winter and we would hit the road in spring, with me driving north and picking him up in New York City.

There is a whole segment to this story that involves Lin and me reconnecting, but I'll save that for another time. I spent the winter living in my van on my folk's property in Sunrise and then moving into a studio cottage in Pompano Beach when the weather got way too warm for me and my dog Ginger. Throughout my Florida stay I was talking to Rich regularly. As karma would have it Rich was

GOD IS

experiencing another GS episode. As Rich got older the episodes became more frequent and severe.

Maybe now's a good time to explain the statement I made earlier, "He might have lived even longer if he wasn't so obsessed with proving he was healthy and didn't put so much stress on his body in the quest to prove that." Rich and I were both into long distance running, read that as "marathon obsessed." There was an instance when the GS flared up rather severely and the best medical thinking was that Rich would not survive this episode. When he miraculously recovered Rich decided he was going to enter and run the New York City Marathon. He ran part of it before giving up, but not soon enough to not seriously affect his body and its ability to resist the GS.

So to continue the narrative, Lin and I lived on opposite coasts of Florida. Lin lived in Sarasota. Each weekend we'd hookup by one of us doing what we called the "Alligator Alley Shuffle." There came a weekend when Lin was having a friend from up north come for a visit and it would not work for me to be present. I was not used to being on my own in Florida and I wasn't sure what to do with myself. I had enough recovery to know not to go to a dance or strip club by myself. I wasn't much of a movie goer either, so I obtained a copy of the local weekly freebie to see what was happening in my area. I saw an announcement of a tea and cookie social at a Vedanta Center not far from where I was living. I was, at that time, growing in my exploration of spirituality. I had heard the term Vedanta but wasn't really sure what it was all about, so I decided to attend. Hell, the cookies would probably be sufficient enough of a reward for my attendance. My second wife didn't call me a cookie wookie for nothing.

When I arrived at the center there was only the hostess present. We sat and talked, drank tea and ate cookies for about an hour. During that time no one showed up and I was given an hour long run down on Vedanta. The telephone rang and my hostess went to answer it. I realized that this was as good as any time to leave, so I made my goodbye and was headed out the door just as this whirlwind pixie of a female was entering. Her energy was so strong, so vibrant and so powerful. In so many ways, this woman's impact upon me was as powerful as Cynthia's (a story yet to be told) but different. I knew immediately that we were not destined to be lovers. She identified herself as Shelly and I introduced myself. We exchanged some small talk. I informed her that there was no one else in attendance and that she was going to be by herself until the hostess got off the telephone. Shelly asked me to stay and continue our conversation. I agreed. I'm not sure how long we talked, but the remainder of our conversation went uninterrupted by the hostess. One of the two things that stayed with me from that conversation was that neither of us had ever been to this center before and that, in all likelihood, we would never be there again. Both of us found out about this social from the same source, the weekly freebie. This "coincidence" takes on even more significance with the memorable second segment of our conversation.

I started telling Shelly about my latest conversation with Rich. I also shared with her how ill he was getting and how I believed that I was destined to become a healer and that my path as a healer was unalterably routed through Rich.

I expressed how I wished I could do something for Rich, even at this distance. Shelly smiled and stated that she knew a way. It was then that I was, conceptually, introduced to Reiki. After the introduction Shelly told me she could give me the first Reiki activation. I agreed and we set up an appointment at Shelly's home office. The fee for the first activation was going to be $199.00.

I arrived at the appointed time and was asked to stand up in the middle of the practice area. Shelly walked around me making motions and chanting softly. I was then asked to lay face up on her massage table. Shelly proceeded to identify six areas of my body, from head to toe. She then explained that these were the first six areas of a client that I would work on. I was then turned over and six more areas were identified. Shelly then informed me that I should spend five minutes Reikiing each of the twelve designated areas thus giving me a chargeable hour's practice. We concluded the session with me being given a series of chants and corresponding visualizations to utilize in the healing practice. When I inquired as to how this was going to help Rich I was informed that distance healing was the next activation. We set up an appointment for three weeks down the road for the second session. Shelly informed me that I was to practice the chanting and visualizations, that I would be tested on them at our next session, and that I should practice the procedure on as many people as I could. My practice participants was a set of one, Lin.

I know this might sound like I was being conned, but every fiber of my being told me this was legitimate and I needed to continue on this path. That the two of us, Shelly and myself, being together at the same time, at a place that neither of us ever was before or would be again, and that Shelly having an answer to my question, was Divinely Synchronistic in its origin.

The second session took place at Shelly's place, again. I was tested as promised. My test consisted of performing Reiki on Shelly. Talk about pressure. Anyway, I passed the test. Shelly then gave me the second set of chants and visualizations that would allow me to send healing over the ethers. I was also given a specifically worded intention to begin the distance healing session with. The fee for this activation was $299.00

Let me clarify a few points at this juncture. First was that I had no intention of using this energy healing technique as a fee based practice. This would go against everything I was coming to believe about healing and doing the Creator's work and was inconsistent with the practices of the teachers I had up until that point. The consistency of that teaching would carry forward through the teachers yet to be acquainted with. As Edgar Cayce, an individual I considered to be one of my teachers even though we had never met in the physical and who had been dead for several decades by this time, said "Original Sin was the use of the Creative Force for selfish purposes."

The second point was that I knew on a deep instinctive level that for me going to Shelly for the activations was like the Cowardly Lion going to the Wizard of Oz for courage. The medal given to the Cowardly Lion was symbolic—that the courage was already there, that the Lion just needed something external to validate it. The activations weren't required. The chants and visualizations were a tool that allowed me to focus my mind so that I would get Ego out of the way and allow the part of me that was the First Cause to flow out unimpeded.

I believe the entire Shelly episode occurred in late April, early May. Lin and I left Florida in late June and headed north. We visited with Rich, as well as Muriel and Charlie, in their condo in Yonkers, New York. It was great to see Muriel and Charlie again. It was not so great to see Rich. He was very sick, his energy was very weak. Rich was in no shape to travel. We agreed to stay in touch and if he got strong enough to travel, we would come back for him. After our visit Lin and I headed north up through New England and into Canada. Our plan was to travel west through Canada stopping in Quebec, Montreal and Toronto before returning to the states via northern Michigan. While we were in Montreal I made contact with Rich and discovered he was doing worse than when we were with him in Yonkers. Lin, bless her sweet, loving compassionate heart had no problem with my needing to reroute our journey so I could work with Rich on his healing. It was time for the rubber to meet the road. If I was meant to be a healer and Rich was the path to that end, then I had to put up or forever shut up. We decided on Woodstock, New York as the place where the healing would take place. We had a good friend, Lauren, who lived in Woodstock who was also in need of a healing of a different variety. Lauren was the first person to tell me that I had healing abilities. Lauren was a friend of Lin's. They worked together for the same company that was a sister to the one I worked for when I cleaned up. It was during that time, during a conversation with Lauren that she informed that I had the gift of healing. Hearing this from Lauren was big. She might have been the most spiritual person I met in early recovery. She had an energy about her that was both soothing yet hurting.

We crossed the border back into the U.S. and headed down the New York State Thruway to Woodstock. We set up residence in The Kenneth L. Wilson Campground just outside of Woodstock. Rich came up a couple of days later and we started three times a day Reiki sessions. We continued this regimen for a few weeks. Rich originally stayed with us in our tent but quickly moved into a room in a house in Woodstock. The sessions continued but decreased to twice a day. After a few weeks Rich looked better, his energy was stronger and he decided he wanted to get out of Woodstock for a while, that he wanted to go back to his folks' place in Yonkers. I knew, on a deep-rooted intuitive level, that Rich was feeling better but that the sessions were not completed. I also knew he would not return for any extended period of time once he left, but it wasn't my place to stop him, only to tell him there was still work to be done for the healing to be permanent. Rich went home and, as reported later, his parents couldn't believe the change in Rich. Rich went to his doctor for an exam and the doctor was amazed that the growth in Rich's abdomen had gotten smaller and softer. Rich came back to Woodstock but only stayed a couple of days. In his mind he was well. As was Rich's pattern, he decided to enter the New York Marathon with the determination to finish it this time. Well he did, but in doing so he put himself in a slow but steady downward spiral that would eventually kill him.

It was because of Rich that I knew I had a gift. It was because of Rich that Lin and I wound up in Woodstock. It was being in Woodstock that facilitated our meeting up with Alvin. It was Alvin who suggested, when we were leaving Woodstock, that if we liked Woodstock and if we found ourselves in the southwest, we should check out Santa Fe, New Mexico. We did wind up in the southwest, we did check out Santa Fe and we've lived here for over 21 years. If you think these sequence of events are a sufficient enough gift from Rich you would be right. However, the gifts didn't end here.

As I stated earlier, there is more to being an addict than consuming large amounts of drugs. Being an addict is about being driven by an almost unstoppable obsession and compulsion that rules an individual's life. For this addict the prominent, but not exclusive, manifestation of addiction was substances. Being an addict meant that I was prone to abuse anything that made me feel good and could distract me from dealing with Phil. Right behind drugs was sex. No sooner were Lin and I settled into life in Santa Fe than my addiction in the form of obsessive sex kicked in. I left Lin due to my behaviors and my best thinking. My best thinking came from a place of self-degradation and low self-esteem. This manifested in the form of, in poker parlance "leaving money on the table." I was in a constant state of belief that there was always something better around the next corner. I didn't trust my ability to make decisions that were for my greater good.

Here is where Rich gave me his most important and final gift. You see, he never recovered from his marathon run and was eventually hospitalized with no hope of ever surviving the hospitalization. I was unaware of all this until I received a call from a mutual friend advising me that Rich had been on life support and that he was being removed from it, and that there was no hope for a recovery. He was given a few hours to live once the life support was removed. As was Rich's way he went about proving the experts wrong one more time. He lasted several days.

Anyway, I was devastated when I received the news. I knew it was going to happen but feeling it intuitively doesn't prepare you for the reality of being told it was happening. Without a moment's hesitation, I called Lin. Not just because she knew Rich but because I knew in my heart of hearts that she was the only person whose shoulder I could cry on and who I wanted to be comforted by. This realization led me to the understanding that I almost destroyed the best possible relationship I could ever have. Lin was soon to be heading out of town for the summer, to work in Yellowstone National Park. From the time of my reaching out to Lin and the time she left for Yellowstone National Park, the two of us spent considerable time discussing the renewed possibility of us. Lin and I spent quite a lot of time talking on the telephone once she arrived at Yellowstone. It was during that time that I sat down with a pen and paper and did a Fourth Step, "Made a searching and fearless moral inventory of ourselves," on my sexually acting out. The insights that this work provided me was immeasurable. I got to meet myself as I had never done before in this area. The Fifth

Step states "Admitted to God, to ourselves and another human being the exact nature of our wrongs." Since the step does not specifically state who that other human being should be, I chose to send the work to Lin. I wanted her to know why I acted the way I did so we could put the past in its place and start working on a new and better us. It worked, we've been together since the Fall of 1995 and I couldn't be more serene or happier than I've been.

The title of this chapter, "Rich Was," needs to be summarized here. It was through my relationship with Rich that I was able to find enough sanctuary to help me survive my teen years. Because of Rich I started the journey of how to heal, myself as well as facilitating it for others, and to verify, to myself if no one else, that I had been blessed with the gift of healing. Because of Rich, Lin and I wound up in Woodstock, which through Alvin led us to Santa Fe from which emanated all sorts of amazing gifts. And, in his passing, Rich showed me what was really important in life: a relationship with a remarkable woman as opposed to being a serial slut. To me this relationship shows that karma is real, that there were way too many gifts and incredible events centered around a single human being, proving to me, without a doubt, that an All Powerful, All Knowing Entity has created a system that allows each and every one of us, if we get out of our own way, to grow spiritually no matter who we were and what we did.

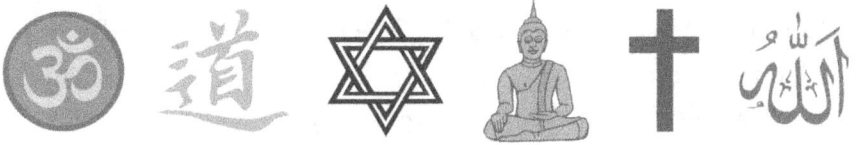

CYNTHIA WAS

I mentioned Cynthia in the previous chapter so I thought I would share our story at this juncture. I was clean for a short period of time when I met Cynthia. I got clean in central New Jersey and even though I was still married and living with Teri, we were, at best, estranged. We were more like housemates than anything else. We lived in separate bedrooms and were basically living together as long as it would take to sell the house we lived in. Teri was a real estate agent and the listing agent for our house. This was done to maximize the amount of money we would get from the sale of the house, since no commission would be paid to the listing agent.

I had lots free time on my hands and I didn't want to spend it at home. Home, one more time, was not a place that brought me peace and comfort. The dynamic between Teri and myself was, basically, constant tension. We lost, for the most part, the ability to be civil with each other. Karma strikes again. Whether it was the home of my parents or the home of my first and/or second wife, I felt like a stranger in a strange land. The only comfortable home I experienced, up until living with Lin, was the period of time between wives that I lived on my own.

As with my childhood I found a couple of places that represented sanctuary to me. One of those places was New Hope, PA which was a pleasant, not too long drive along some basically undeveloped back roads. New Hope is situated in Lower Bucks County on the Delaware River and was a funky little artist/biker town when I first discovered it. In the closing words of the Eagles "Last Resort" written by Don Henley,

They called it paradise, I don't know why.
You call someplace paradise, kiss it goodbye.

Well over time New Hope was kissed goodbye, it became a tourist attraction and the town lost, for me at least, its funk and its charm. They closed down the sex shop, they created smoked glass atrium fronts on a few of the restaurants and gift shops, selling touristy junk, took over for the artists stores.

I encountered Cynthia for the first time in New Hope. I was strolling Main Street, doing what I enjoyed, people watching. During my first marriage I would get loaded and head into Manhattan to watch people. Sometimes I would hang out in Central Park, sometimes at the Metropolitan Museum of Art. Sometimes I took a camera with me, most times I didn't. Hiding in a crowd was a special skill of mine. I hid in crowds of a million or more people. Anyway, I'm walking Main Street when I have this intense energetic feeling. I look around and sense and see this strikingly tall, sharp-dressed woman walking in my direction. I knew I had to meet this individual.

Allow me to digress here. As spiritual beings (souls) we choose our incarnations, the karmic lessons we get the opportunity to meet ourselves in and who our helpmates are. If our karmic lessons are in early childhood we don't have to identify our helpmates, they are situated where they need to be, such as our parents, siblings, teachers etc.... When our helpmates are set up to meet us later in life we need a mechanism to identify the individual, as they do us. That mechanism is that vibratory feeling we get when we meet someone for the first time. Because our culture, for the most part, doesn't believe in karma and reincarnation and because we are love starved, when we sense this signal we interpret it to be romantic in nature. Instead of meeting a helpmate we have met our soul mate. This is not to imply that a helpmate and a soul mate can't be contained in the same individual. They most certainly are. It's just that we will meet so many more helpmates than soul mates and approaching each of these individuals as a soul mate usually gets in the way of the karmic lesson, the gift they bring to us. It can so cloud the picture that our Higher Self will have to scramble to put us in a position to have another chance at the planned for karmic lesson.

Since I'm wandering far off course let's wander a little further. Let's talk about love. I believe that our teacher, Ego, as part of one of our most, if not our most important lesson, has us convinced that love is an emotion. As long as we attempt to emote love we will always experience limits. As long as we experience limits we are not experiencing love because love has no limits. As long as our belief that the source of love eludes us by deluding us into seeking in all the wrong places, we stay searching and focused on the human realm as opposed to the spiritual realm. Love is not an emotion, it is a spiritual demonstration. Ego is solely about fear, about lack. These are the qualities that teach us what isn't working in our lives. Spirit is the opposite, it is solely about love and abundance. These are the qualities that teach us what is working in our lives. If both entities were capable of teaching the same lessons, we wouldn't need the free will that gives us the ability to choose between the clear distinctions of Spirit and Ego. Without the free-will choice, how would we ever learn enough to evolve enough to become a companion with God?

Back to Cynthia. At this point in my journey I didn't have the understandings expressed in the previous paragraphs. So, when I sensed Cynthia walking towards me I was in love. I was intent on introducing myself. Just before we would have been face to face Cynthia turned and entered a dry goods store. The store had a porch, which I made good use of. I planted myself on the railing where the door and the steps met up. I was willing to wait there for eternity, if that was what it took for the opportunity to introduce myself to this woman. Talk about being love starved. The moment arrived when she exited the store and I approached her. I immediately told her that I felt her walking in my direction, that her energy was so powerful, and I just had to meet her. Cynthia didn't seem to have a problem with this move. We chatted for a few moments, long enough to find out that Cynthia was visiting a friend here in New Hope and that she lived in Florida. My best thinking was, there goes happily ever after, maybe we can have a short, torrid affair. I invited Cynthia to join me for lunch, to which she agreed. Little did I know what doors this invitation was opening.

We made small talk during the short walk to the restaurant. Cynthia shared that she was leaving for home tomorrow. This was going to be a much shorter affair than I anticipated. Once we were seated and ordered our beverages and appetizers Cynthia asked me to allow her to hold one of the rings I was wearing. You see, back then, my Leo was very strong. I wore four rings on each hand, all of them silver. I was never a gold person, maybe something from another life. I removed the ring on my right pinkie finger and handed it to her. The ring was my favorite. I bought it during my first trip to Mexico. It was the head of the Mexican Sun God, Huitzilopochtli. Being on the cusp between Cancer and Leo I had the Sun God (Leo) on my right hand pinkie and a Moonstone (Cancer) on the pinkie of my left hand.

Cynthia wrapped her hand around the ring and went into, what I would say, was a trance for a few seconds. Then, just like the woman in Martinique, Cynthia started to tell me about my conflicts with my father, the path my life had taken and the troubles with my current marriage. When Cynthia was finished revealing my life back at me I asked her how she did what she just did. Cynthia explained that what she did was called Psychometry. That she was not only able to give psychic readings, she was also able to locate missing children, alive or dead, by holding an object of theirs. Cynthia went on to share that she did this quite frequently in Europe, that the police there were much more open to utilizing the gifts that Cynthia possessed. On the other hand the police in our country wanted no part of her ability. Cynthia stated that she never profited from her gift; the police in Europe would pay her expenses but she would never accept anything more than expenses. I asked Cynthia how long she had this gift. She explained that she was born with her gifts, that she came from a long line of psychics, each manifesting different gifts. She then shared that she had two visitations from Jesus, one as a child, the other as a teen.

The first one occurred in what Cynthia described as a place between the awake state and the dream state. Cynthia was being attacked by a demon and Jesus showed up and dispelled the demon. The second visit wasn't quite as dramatic. Jesus showed up in that same overlapping state of consciousness, stating to Cynthia that he would always be there for her. We spent hours at the restaurant talking. When it came time for Cynthia to go she gave me her address and phone number and told me if I was ever in need, to call and if I was ever going to be in her part of Florida, to let her know. Little did I know what lessons Cynthia would have to teach me.

Not too long after my encounter with Cynthia a young child went missing in Perth Amboy, New Jersey, a town not far from where I lived. I had this intuitive sense that I should call Cynthia. I asked her if she could locate a child without holding an object of theirs. Cynthia responded that she could but the results weren't as accurate and reliable as when she was holding an item belonging to the child. I read Cynthia the article in the newspaper and after a short silence Cynthia described a location where the child's body could be found. I called the police and identified myself and why I was calling. The officer listened to what I had to say, took down the information and thanked me for my interest. Basically, just like Cynthia had experienced, local police had no room in their discipline for psychics. Somewhere down the road the child's body was found in an area that matched Cynthia's description.

During the time I was living on the east coast of Florida, before I met Shelly, I made contact with Cynthia. She invited me to her house. During our reunion the telephone rang and Cynthia answered it. When she returned she explained that the call was from a local Pastor and that she had a client coming over. I asked if she was going to locate a missing child. Cynthia explained that she possessed another gift that we hadn't touched on. Cynthia went on to state that she had the ability, by laying her hands on others, to heal them from their physical afflictions. She went on to relate that there was an underground network of some of the more liberal thinking clergy who referred to Cynthia individuals who had exhausted all possible avenues of healing.

As with her locating children, Cynthia wouldn't accept payment from the individuals she facilitated healings for. I saw the woman upon her arrival and again after her treatment and she was like two different individuals. I didn't inquire as to the healing but the physical presentation, as well as the energetic feel convinced me that this was another powerful gift that Cynthia was endowed with.

Over the next month or so Cynthia and I spent a lot of time together. Cynthia's source of income was as a home-based antique dealer. One day I went with Cynthia to an estate sale. Cynthia bought a couple of pieces, made arrangements for them to be delivered; and she also bought a tall, sparse, potted plant that we were going to take home with us. Cynthia drove a Chrysler convertible. Cynthia put the top down and drove while I sat shotgun with the plant between my legs. My job was to keep the plant as low down as possible so the leaves wouldn't be blown away. With the plant's wellbeing as our number-one priority, Cynthia drove home slowly, using the single lane back roads as our route. Along our route there were stretches of road that didn't allow passing. During one of those stretches there was a car behind us who was in a big hurry, riding our tail and honking their horn repeatedly. Cynthia refused to be hurried and held her speed. We came to a traffic light that turned red upon our arrival. The driver of the car behind us jumped out of his car and came at Cynthia angry and animated. Cynthia reached into her handbag and, as the irate driver arrived at her door, pulled out this huge gun and pointed it in his face, while asking, in a calm, gentle voice, "do you really want to complain about my driving?" By the look on the driver's face I would guess that he wet his pants. He backed away quietly as the light turned green and Cynthia pulled away, smiling, calmly placing the gun back in her bag. The driver of the car behind us remained out of sight for the remainder of our time on that road. The lesson this episode held for me is that possessing gifts of the spirit doesn't mean the possessor is in line for sainthood, that the gifts are just that, gifts from the Divine, while a spiritual life is based upon a regular spiritual practice.

One day I arrived at Cynthia's house and was alarmed by Cynthia's energy and physical appearance. Cynthia stated that she was experiencing strong abdominal pains. I offered to do for Cynthia what she had been doing for so many others, the laying on of healing hands. Cynthia laid down on her couch and I sat alongside of her. I placed my hands on her abdomen and proceeded to attempt to squeeze out as much healing energy as I possessed. Part of this effort was driven by my desire to validate my being a healer along with a significant part being my feelings for Cynthia and my desire for her to be pain free. This exercise lasted maybe five minutes before Cynthia brought it to a close stating that there was nothing happening. I was crushed. Cynthia must have felt my disappointment because she immediately stood up, wrapped her arms around me and gave me a powerful hug. I reciprocated the hug. It lingered longer than normal, I didn't want to disentangle. As we stood there holding each other Cynthia stated "there it is." When I asked "there what is," Cynthia responded "the healing energy." Here was another important lesson that Cynthia was the vehicle for. In order to channel the Creator's healing energy I needed to be detached from the results. Attaching to the results inserted self-will into the process and self-will can and does block the First Cause's healing energy.

For a variety of reasons, not important to this narrative, Cynthia and I drifted apart after the above episode. The last time I contacted Cynthia was probably a decade later. I was involved with a missing child's family and reached out to Cynthia to see if she could be of help. Like the other incident regarding a missing child, Cynthia's information was of no use. This was due to the mother of the missing child refusing to accept her child's death, she was only interested in finding her child alive. During this connection Cynthia shared with me that over the course of the intervening years her abdominal condition continued to worsen. She stated that she went to numerous traditional doctors and a few psychic healers with no relief being obtained. Healing was finally obtained when Cynthia traveled to Brazil and had a session with John of God. Cynthia reported that John of God repeatedly stuck his hand into her abdomen and pulled out several large handfuls of black toxic material. Cynthia was advised by John of God that the toxicity was the result of all the healings she had performed and that, if she didn't want a repeat of what brought her to him she would need to cease her healing work. Cynthia appeared to be okay with this and limited the utilization of her gifts to Psychometry.

The collective lessons that Cynthia facilitated for me deeply reinforced that there was nothing impossible in God's universe. That in The Creator's universe all things are connected and that as human beings we are capable of tapping into that Divine Providence and producing results that transcend our supposed human limitations. I've stopped believing in luck, coincidence, random occurrences, even miracles. These are just words humans have created in an attempt to explain away God's presence in our lives. Every time we explain away The First Cause's work instead of crediting it, we diminish The Divine and make ourselves that much smaller. How can the examples of Divine Synchronicity I've already shared, coupled with the ones I will continue to share not constitute, in legalistic terms, "A preponderance of evidence"? I am sure that as you are reading this, numerous examples of your own experience of Divine Synchronicity are coming to the forefront of your consciousness.

God knew how to get my attention. The Great Mystery presented me with what appeared to be a random, hopefully sexual, encounter which turned into my being taught lessons I didn't even know I needed to know. All these lessons were and continue to be essential in forwarding me on the path I am currently walking. **GOD IS**.

TERI WAS

Teri was my second wife. Our meeting was, without a doubt, karmic. It happened during my active addiction. I was invited to a party by Alice, a friend of a former sex buddy. Sex buddies were my way of not having to be alone with myself and not having to commit to being with any one individual. My basic belief was that I was incapable of sustaining a healthy, normal relationship so I avoided doing so at all costs. As soon as the concept of an exclusive relationship was run up the flag pole I ran. There was always another couple or three buddies ready to fill in the vacancy. I was, for lack of a better term, a chronic slut.

Somehow, a couple or so months prior to this party, through the drug-induced fog that blanketed my life, I had come to the realization that I had lost all sense of discriminatory taste when it came to sex partners. I took a vow of celibacy. These were desperate times. As my sexually acting-out decreased, my consumption of drugs increased.

As a general rule I hated any gathering that consisted of more than two other individuals. It reminded me of family gatherings during childhood in which I was never comfortable. However, my ever-increasing state of horniness overcame my fear of gatherings. This act of courage was in part fueled by the hostess of the party, Alice. I had met Alice when I was with her friend, the aforementioned sex buddy. I attempted to hit on Alice but was turned down because I was in a relationship with Alice s friend. Alice reeked of sex. I had a classification system back then. There were women who held no sexual appeal for me, neither physically nor energetically. It was bedding a number of women in this category that convinced me I needed to go celibate. The next category was a woman who had a body made for a brothel and a libido made for a convent. An equal category was a libido made for a brothel and a body made for convent, whatever that means. The most desirable category, the one Alice personified was having a body and a libido made for a brothel.

Even though I had my sights set on Alice, that didn't totally remove my aversion to gatherings. In order to get through the night, I upped my intake of mood and mind-altering substances substantially. I arrived at Alice's place early, hoping to lay the foundation for an evening of pleasure. Unfortunately, Alice was a last minute kind of gal and there were a handful of preparations still to be done. Alice suggested that I get a drink and relax. That was absolutely the last suggestion I needed to hear but I took it anyway. Being who I was, the drink I took was not of the social size; you probably could have served a number of people with it. The last thing I remember was sitting down in a corner of the living room in this padded armchair that rocked. The next thing I remember was coming to, to this powerful energy tingling my entire being. I looked around and saw the source of this feeling. There was this impressive, black-haired, dark olive-complexioned woman with a body designed for sex and an energy that screamed power and sensuality, standing in the doorway. She was wearing white slacks and a black shirt. I was wearing black slacks and a white shirt. As I absorbed this woman's impact on me and the feelings she triggered, another guy approached her and started talking to her. I knew I needed to act immediately but I was still wasted and I wasn't sure I could string together a coherent sentence. The only way I can explain what happened next was that Divine Presence straightened me up sufficiently to be able to walk and then talk. I walked over to where the two were talking, inserted myself in the conversation and rapidly went on to dominate it, cutting out my competition. I guess I was able to get away with this because I was over a head taller and outweighed him by a significant amount. I introduced myself and the woman introduced herself as Teri.

I need to share the significance of our attire at that initial meeting. It was related to me at a later date that Teri and I had mutual astrological sun/moon oppositions. What this means is that my sun was 180 degrees opposite Teri's moon and Teri's sun was 180 degrees opposite my moon. Any two people who share just one opposition have a powerful connection, with the bearer of the sun being the dominant individual in the relationship. When there is a mutual sun/moon opposition, the attraction is overpowering with the dominance being shared. So there we were, my black slacks opposite Teri's white ones and my white shirt opposite Teri's black one. Are you starting to doubt the concepts of luck, coincidence, random occurrences, even miracles yet?

One of the energetic oppositions that Teri and I brought into our relationship was that we triggered each other in our parental-induced vulnerabilities. Teri's way of dealing with me when I was angry, which was almost my constant state of being, reminded me of my father. Teri withdrew. Teri's withdrawal would feed my anger which, in turn, fed Teri's continued withdrawal. You see, my anger reminded Teri of her mother and how her mother dealt with life and with Teri. These episodes triggered Teri to deal with me as she dealt with her mother. Which in turn led me to act out in whatever way I could come up with so that I could get Teri to respond to me. Most of what I would come up with was totally dysfunctional and, more than likely, violent. There were, however, equally important lessons Teri was destined to teach me.

One of Teri's friends, Ginger, was one of the first licensed astrologers in the U.S. I met her and her husband Donald, on my second date with Teri. It was then that I learned about sun/moon oppositions and my sharing them with Teri. I also had my sense of something bigger/greater, behind/supporting the world I lived in/on reinforced. Ginger was able to tell me my story, almost identically to the way the woman in Martinique and Cynthia did. Ginger also told me that my chart showed that I was destined to be surrounded by women. This fed that addict mentality of mine, giving me an excuse to continue my sluttish ways. I even created a myth in support of this astrologically-based inclination. I told people that being a slut was the karmic balance I was here to experience in compensation for being sacrificed as a virgin in a previous Mayan existence. A clear example of a little knowledge being a dangerous thing.

You might be asking yourself, "Why would I, believing what I did about my ability to successfully sustain a relationship, enter into a relationship?" The answer is simple. First of all, I came to believe that the problem with my first marriage was my first wife's fault. I had been in numerous quasi-relationships since my first marriage ended, and my anger and violence never reared its ugly head. What I learned later on down the road was it never reared its head because I was loaded most of the time, and because the relationships were with people who didn't mean enough to me for me to lose it with them.

Secondly, fueled by my minute but growing metaphysical beliefs I was sure that Teri and I were "Soul Mates." Our early relationship bore that out. We started living together soon thereafter and every aspect of our relationship was incredible. The smoothness turned rough almost immediately after we got married. I believe the change of our status changed our definitions and expectations of each other. The things that I did and didn't do took on greater significance for Teri as did the way Teri reacted to and dealt with me. Before we knew it, our great love became a toxic battlefield. I thought Teri was my validation, my salvation. That was an unrecognized but very prevalent perception on my part. Teri was to prove all those experiences from childhood on were not really about me. To meet myself as the angry, vulnerable, rage-filled Phil of old shattered me. It drove me deeper into my self-medication which drove me further away from myself, Teri and any healing we might have been able to facilitate. The realization that those fears were real drove me deeper into anger. Like with my father, no matter what I did, no matter my intentions, the wounds grew deeper, the fears grew greater. By God's Grace and my actions, may I never, ever have to re-experience that state of madness, in this life or any other. Karma be damned.

In Twelve Step Spirituality the Ninth Step is about making amends. How does one make amends for inflicting the amount of pain that I had? The only amends I could make was a Divinely inspired statement. I simply, but sincerely, told Teri that there was never, ever, anything she had done that warranted the way I treated her. Teri's response was that she didn't believe a word I said.

We stayed out of contact until about a decade later when Teri sought me out to let me know that my last running buddy, Steve, had died from the disease of addiction. During the ensuing conversation I asked Teri why she stayed with me for so long. Her response was like a stake through the heart. Teri stated that she had deeply loved me and that I had convinced her that it was all her fault. There I was meeting myself as my father, meeting the fear, anger and rage that had been imprinted on me so long ago. I took that opportunity to reiterate my amends. This time Teri was receptive to them and we had, what I would define, as a lengthy, healing conversation. My hope, my prayer is that Teri has been able to move on and create a life for herself that is as, if not more than, rewarding and fulfilling than the life I have now.

Teri And The Reverend

Teri was the catalyst/focal point for my having so many experiences and meeting so many people that would kick-start me on this path of having a spiritual awakening. I'm not sure of the sequence of the experiences that I had, so I will just write about them as they come to the forefront of my psyche.

The first experience that comes to mind was the Reverend. I don't know if he had the credentials for the title or just adopted it. He was a psychic who lived in a little house in Edison, New Jersey. The Rev. held open house psychic readings twice a week. People would line up on his porch, outside his home, down the block and around the corner to get in for a reading. It was the kind of line you would expect for a first run blockbuster at the local movie theater. Prior to entering the house there would be a donation box at the door, the suggested donation was $2.00. Upon entering the house you were greeted by a woman, who I was told was the Rev.'s wife. She would guide you to your seat. The readings were held in their living room. The room would be reconfigured, holding three rows of four chairs each with a podium at the front of the room. When you entered the room, the seats at the back were vacant. As each person completed their reading they would get up and leave, and the congregation would move forward, refilling the front rows. When it was your turn for a reading you would simply say, "good evening Rev." The Rev. would then greet you and give you your reading. The reading lasted only a few minutes. When it was over you were allowed to ask a question and, on a rare occasion, you were allowed a second clarifying question. Teri and I were there once for the start of the session. The Rev. would be led out to the podium by his wife, his eyes closed. Once behind the podium the Rev. would hold up both hands above his head, palms outward, the fingers on both hands spread in the Vulcan greetings configuration. He would remain silent for a couple of minutes and his wife would then indicate his readiness to begin.

The times I went with Teri I always entered with her but I never received a reading. When Teri was finished with her reading I would stand and exit with her. The reason I avoided the reading was a fear of knowing what the future held. Being a using addict at the time I was afraid of everything. My fear was rooted in the belief that there wasn't anything positive in my life nor would there be in the future, so why would I want to know what was awaiting me. I was better off ignorant than informed.

I did witness Teri's readings and I was impressed. I also talked with other congregants about the accuracy of their readings and was advised that they were accurate. Prior to our first attending the readings, Teri informed me that my soon-to-be presence in her life was foretold by the Rev. According to Teri I was described by the Rev. both physically and temperamentally. During one of the earlier readings of Teri's that I witnessed, the Rev. advised her to not try to change me, that I wouldn't react well to that, and that it would be the cause of our separating. This reading was dead on. As I recall it, and Teri might recall it differently, while we were living together, but not married, our life, from my perspective was idyllic. Once we got married, the definition of my role as a husband changed radically from my definition as a live-in lover. It was like a switch had been thrown. The things that used to be acceptable were no longer so. How I did things was now being scrutinized and corrected. This triggered my anger which triggered Teri's withdrawal, which created a regularly repeating downward spiral to our love and our relationship. I remember asking Teri repeatedly, why she wasn't adhering to the Rev.'s advice. I don't remember ever getting an answer to that question.

TERI AND EDGAR CAYCE

Over the course of my spiritual journey I have been blessed with many wonderful teachers. Some have been in the physical, some have been in the Spirit and some have been through the teachings they have left behind. Of all my lessons that came through the teachings that have been left behind, the greatest impact on my soul was the teachings of Edgar Cayce. Those lessons began with my second wife Teri. Probably the greatest spiritual gift that Teri gave me was introducing me to Edgar Cayce. Teri was a member of Edgar Cayce's Association for Research and Enlightenment (A.R.E.) when I met her. She would receive newsletters regularly and would sometimes share their contents with me. Teri also participated in a few research groups. The ones that I remember were a dream research group and a meditation research group. However, what really grabbed my attention was Teri's utilization of the information in the Dr. Riley book titled *Good Health Through Drugless Therapy*.

I've read that Edgar Cayce was credited with being the Father of Holistic healing. If that is true then Dr. Riley's book is the scripture. Anyway, Teri was taking an aerobics class on Friday evenings. One night she came home with an ankle the size of a grapefruit. Teri stated that she landed improperly and the ankle snapped so loudly that the entire class heard it over the music. At the time Teri was employed as a Chiropractic Assistant. The doctor she worked for was more of a sports medicine guy than a pure chiropractor. We called him, told him what happened and was instructed to meet him, immediately, at his office. Once at the office the doctor examined the ankle and stated that it didn't appear to be broken and was more than likely severely sprained. However, it was too swollen to be x-rayed and only x-rays could determine for sure what had happened to the ankle. The doctor gave Teri some crutches, instructed her to stay off the ankle as much as possible, and he would x-ray it on Monday provided the swelling decreased sufficiently. Just as a point of reference, at this point Teri couldn't put any pressure on the injured ankle.

When we arrived home Teri instructed me to gather up the following items; apple cider vinegar, kosher salt, a pure cotton cloth, a plastic bag, two strings and a glass baking dish. Teri explained that these were the necessary ingredients for a healing pack as outlined in the Dr. Riley book. Teri said that she had utilized this procedure with her daughters with great success.

Teri directed me to cover the bottom of the baking pan with apple cider vinegar, to soak the cotton cloth in the vinegar, to pour the kosher salt onto one side of the cloth and to wrap the cloth around the swollen ankle, salt side to the skin. I next wrapped the cloth with the plastic bag and tied both ends with the strings. Teri stated that she would sleep with this on her ankle for three nights. By the time Monday morning came Teri carried the crutches to the doctor's office. Her ankle was still swollen a bit, but the color was almost normal and she was able to walk on it like nothing had ever happened.

I had the opportunity, not too long thereafter, to apply the same treatment to myself. While playing basketball I came down with a rebound, landing on someone's foot and twisted my ankle fairly severely. Just like I had done for Teri, I did for myself and after three nights of going to bed smelling like a salad, I was able to walk as if nothing happened.

Over and above the healing I witnessed and experienced, which was damn impressive, I was being opened up to a world that existed beyond my ability to sense. I started reading books based upon the

Cayce readings. I started reading the newsletters as well. And I started to get involved with a group of Teri's friends who were into, what was termed during that time, New Age Spirituality. In some ways they were the evolutionary remains of the Hippie movement.

As I was driven to learn more about Cayce, Teri suggested I read a biography on Cayce's life titled *There Is A River* by Thomas Sergue. It should come as no surprise that Teri had this book on her shelf. Cayce's biography expanded my horizons with regard to the existence of other realms of reality, as well as bringing to the forefront of my consciousness a deep rooted connection to Cayce. I started to digest Cayce addictively. The first book I read on the Cayce readings was the Dr. Riley book. It became a reference book that has always been with me. The first non-holistic healing book of Cayce's readings that I read was *Edgar Cayce's Story of Jesus* by Jeffrey Furst. At the time I picked it up I wasn't really familiar with the speech pattern that was prevalent in Cayce's readings. Reading and digesting lengthy Cayce discourses was similar to reading The Bible or Shakespeare for the first time. The rhythm of expression was as alien to me as a foreign language. I have since read dozens of books written about a particular, singular subject from the Cayce readings without a single one of them quoting directly from the readings as much as Furst did.

The first time I picked up the Jesus book I made it to about page 20 before I put it down as indecipherable. My second attempt got me to around page 50, before arriving at the same conclusion. Driven by Divine Wisdom, I can't believe anything but that could move me to return to this book a third time; I read the entire book. For the first time in my life I had an explanation of Jesus and life as a spiritual unfolding that made sense, not just on an intellectual level but that resonated at the level of my soul.

Teri And The Tarot

Along with Teri's embracing of psychic readers, she was also into astrology and Tarot card readings. I had never experienced the Tarot before. Teri owned a few different Tarot decks. The one that called to me was the Egyptian deck. As I inspected it I felt guided to work with it. I had no idea how to utilize the deck, so I asked Teri for guidance. Her guidance came in the form of advising me to get a book on Tarot. I did, immediately.

The book, whose name and author escapes me, gave me the history of Tarot readings and an explanation as to the meaning of the cards. I started doing readings for anyone who would sit with me long enough to complete a reading. I gravitated to one particular formation for the read. This layout utilized nine cards. Five were on the left side with four making up a circle which engulfed the fifth card. The other four were lined up straight to the right of the circle. In this configuration eight of the nine cards had a polarity. If they were turned over face top side up, the cards had a positive meaning. If they were turned over face bottom side down, the cards had a negative meaning. The card in the center of the circle was placed on its vertical side, laying horizontally. This card was neutral. I started off using the book as a guide to the interpretation of the cards. It soon became clear to me that the book offered multiple and sometimes contradictory meanings to the cards. More and more I followed my intuitive sense interpreting the cards and the feedback I received attested to the accuracy of the read. What I later took away from this was that I was reading the individual not the cards.

I gave four readings, two groupings of two, about six weeks apart that I don't believe I will ever forget. The first two readings were done on New Year's Eve for a friend of Teri and her daughter. I read for the daughter first. It was a pretty normal type reading. The only memorable part was that the top card in the row, the future card, was the card of Death. In Tarot the death card doesn't always imply that someone was going to die. More often than not, it meant that radical change was approaching. When I finished the daughter's reading I proceeded to read for the mother. Here is where the reading turned strange. The mother had six of the eight directionally relevant cards in the negative facing direction. This included the death card that was also in the future position. I gave the mom a vanilla interpretation of the cards, all the while having these nagging dread feelings knocking at my door. Once the readings were concluded our two guests left. No sooner did they leave, than I became deeply ill. I wound up being bedridden for three days. I later on learned that mom was diagnosed with cancer of the lymph nodes. As it turned out she did recover but her life was never the same afterwards.

The second set of readings took place on Valentine's Day. We had arranged to spend the evening with our married friends Helen and Steve. They were both aware that I was doing Tarot readings and requested that I bring my cards and read for the both of them. Their readings were almost identical to the mother/daughter readings I gave New Year's Eve. Helen, the wife, resided in the daughter's position while Steve resided in the mother's position. The only significant difference was that Steve's reading had one more negative card than the mother had. Shortly after the reading Teri and I departed for home. From Helen and Steve's residence in South Brunswick, New Jersey we drove north on U.S. Highway 1. I was the driver. In order to get to our place, which was also in South Brunswick, we had to go west across the highway. In order to make this turn we had to take a jug handle at the traffic light. When the light turned green we left the jug handle and started crossing the Highway. As we crossed the south bound lane we were struck by a car that went through the red light. We were hit on the passenger side front wheel panel. We were hit with so much force that we were turned southbound and pushed into the east bound lane where we were struck by a vehicle heading west bound to turn north. This car struck us on the passenger side rear door. God was sure looking after Teri and me, especially Teri, since she was on the impact side both times and neither hit was directly at her. Shortly thereafter I was able to put one and one together and realize that two equaled that I was doing Tarot card readings unprotected. Since I had no idea how to protect myself, which was to come later, I wrapped up the cards in a silk cloth and put them away in a drawer until such time as I was able to protect myself.

GOD IS

Another aspect of the story of Shelly and Reiki, as I related in the "Rich Was" section, was the realization that, based on my Tarot card experiences, if I were going to be interacting with other people's energy as a healer I needed to learn how to protect myself from the energies I would encounter. I'll never forget the day I was sitting in my rented bungalow contemplating how I was going to protect myself when a gentle voice in my head gave me the following prayer: "God, thank you for allowing me to facilitate the healing of X (the name of whomever I was working on) and to allow me to not hold onto their energy but to pass it through me to you where it will neutralized."

For quite a while I would silently say the prayer before starting any healing session I engaged in. After that, I came to know that as long as I was doing the Creator's work, I would not be affected by the energies I came into contact with. With that belief being solid, I no longer had to say the prayer before sessions. Behind this belief I started instructing the individuals I was working on to send me their pain during our sessions. Since the time I was given the prayer I have not been affected by the energies of the individuals I worked on.

The intention of returning to the Tarot left me when two understandings were given to me, almost simultaneously. The first was that utilizing a Tarot deck was limiting; that the real dynamic of the reading was one soul connecting with another soul. The second realization, which was an extension of the first one, came a little further down the road. It was that one didn't have to lay hands on or have hands hover near an individual in order to transmit energy. That teaching as a counselor would serve just as effectively as any other method. That the healing energy of the practitioner can be transmitted orally and can be received aurally. The ultimate lesson was that the physical body encompassing the Soul can be either a transmitter or a receiver.

I've used and will continue to use the phrase "being given." I should probably explain what meanings I attach to that phrase. Early on in my journey I believed I was intuiting information based upon an intellectual process combining experience, observation and spiritual study. As the Path unfolded before me I came to believe that the source of the information was karmic in its origins; that I entered this plane with the volume of my spiritual knowledge turned up, so to speak. You see, God Loves all of Its children equally and unconditionally and supports us in all our karmic endeavors. If my karmic blueprint was to learn how to deal with fame and adulation, I might have entered as a world class athlete or an extraordinarily talented musician. In order to walk that karmic path and meet myself, the volume would be turned up in the necessary skill sets.

Where my beliefs currently stand is that I have a Spirit Master that guides me and provides me with the appropriate information for any given situation. This arrangement was facilitated by one of my most important teachers, Maulana. There will be more about our relationship later on in this narrative.

Teri And Recovery

During the time frame encompassed by the previous three segments about Teri I was very active in my addictions. Teri, during that time was, what was known back then as, a New Ager. Teri was part of a group of people who met regularly at each other's homes. They were very into all the latest trends that made up and was constantly transforming the New Age landscape at the time. They met regularly to discuss spiritual topics, watch spiritual movies or listen to a guest speaker; and loved participating in non-religious ceremonies.

It was at one of the few gatherings that I attended that I met Carl. Carl was of Irish decent and about my age and height. Carl had an energy about him that was both calm and gentle. I gravitated to him more than anyone else in the group. Carl was very open with me about his past drinking problems. He was also very forthright with me about recognizing my drug problem. Carl never put me down for my problems, never treated me differently when I was loaded.

My abstinence started because of Carl. The date August 17, 1987, was to be this landmark event known as the "Harmonic Convergence." The Harmonic Convergence was an astrological event wherein the sun, the moon and six of the eight planets in our solar system aligned with each other to form a grand trine. It was also supposed to mark the end of a millennia, plus a negative cycle, and the start of an equally long positive cycle.

There was a married couple in the group who were the unofficial leaders of the group. They had a big house on a large plot of land. Most of the gatherings took place at their home because it was capable of holding the whole group comfortably. So it was natural that an event as important as the Harmonic Convergence be held at their house. Among all the planned happenings was to be a fire ceremony. Carl volunteered for and was designated to build the fire and assure its continuance. The next time I saw Carl he asked me if I would assist him in his sacred duty. I was blown away. I couldn't remember the last time I was asked to be a part of something so special to someone. Of course I said yes. On the spur of the moment I informed Carl that to both show my appreciation for the request and to honor his beliefs, I would not use for the day. The last time I got loaded was August 16, 1987. My clean date is August 17, 1987. It took a while longer for me to achieve any recovery.

I delineate between being clean and being in recovery. Being clean is a destination. One is either using or they are not. Being in recovery is a journey, one that one embarks on infinite times during the course of the day.

Carl suggested to me at some point during the day of the Harmonic Convergence that, since I abstained for a day, I might want to give abstinence a try. I so wanted to be like Carl, to be at peace with the world the way he was that I agreed to give abstinence a try. You see, I needed some peace in my life. The drugs weren't working like they used to. They weren't quieting my mind like they used to. "Used to" should not be read as resembling anything that could be construed as current. I had been experiencing, for years, what is clinically known as tolerance. My mind and my mood were only being minimally altered and the duration was getting shorter and shorter. I was using more and more, and getting less and less out of it. I became a mixologist, mixing ungodly combinations of drugs in the hope of quieting my mind and easing the knot in my gut. I had stopped using to alter my consciousness and had been using to go straight through blackout to pass out. So I was a prime candidate to give abstinence a try.

At this point in my life I was totally ignorant of the clinical definitions of alcoholism and drug addiction. You see, growing up in New York City I was given and had observed some very precise definitions of alcoholism and drug addiction.

There is a place on lower Manhattan that is known as the Bowery. During the late 50's and early 60's there resided in the Bowery individuals known as Bowery Bums. They were the individuals, mostly male, who cleaned the windows of your car as you exited the Brooklyn Battery Tunnel and was stopped by the traffic light. They came equipped, each with their own squeegees and cleaning fluid, and performed their services whether you wanted them to or not. Their goal, obviously, was to receive a tip for their service. The money collected was used to purchase liquor. Anyway, there was a time when the police were finding Bowery Bums dead on the streets with black or brown rings around their lips. It was determined that they were attempting to suck the alcohol out of shoe polish paste, hence the rings, and that they were dying from the lead poisoning that ensued because they were ingesting the lead along with the alcohol from the polish. I never sucked alcohol from shoe polish paste, therefore, I could not be an alcoholic. I may have drunk mouthwash and, on occasion, vanilla extract, but it never dawned on me that it wasn't what I consumed but how much I needed to consume it that mattered.

Regarding being a drug addict, that definition was as equally distorted. The definition I had, and I'm not sure where I obtained it, was that a drug addict was a black jazz musician shooting heroin. Since I wasn't shooting dope, I couldn't carry a tune even if I had a reinforced shopping bag, and I was white I couldn't be a drug addict. The fact that I did whatever I could to get and stay loaded didn't have any significance. My disease informed me that smoking banana skin strings, which didn't work, huffing glue, paint, gasoline or Carbona

Cleaning Fluid wasn't a sign of addiction. It was getting high, which was different.

There was a time during my early using when Monsanto came out with a consumer packaged version of monosodium glutamate (MSG) called Accent. It was advertised with cartoon visuals showing a chicken clucking loudly or a cow strongly mooing or a pig oinking passionately. The tag line for each of these commercials was "Accent brings out the flavor of …." I adopted the tag line morphing it to "drugs bring out the flavor in Phil." Our ego will distort whatever it can in order to convince us that self-destruction is beneficial.

While we are on the subject of drug use, I feel I should explain why I never used needles during my career as an addict. I believe God sent me a messenger early in my using career to dissuade me from using the needle. God knew that I was going to use with an inexhaustible appetite and that shooting drugs would mean my death. The messenger took the form of Stu. Stu was the son of one of my dad's childhood neighborhood friends who lived in the same neighborhood as we did. Stu was a couple of years older than I was, and if it weren't for our fathers being friends Stu and I would probably have had nothing more than a nod of the head, "hi there" relationship. However, because of the old neighborhood connection our fathers had we wound up doing things together like going to a ball game, Yankees of course, or shooting pool. There came a day when Stu and I were hanging out without our fathers when Stu asked me if I was getting high. When I responded to the affirmative, Stu informed me that if he ever heard that I was shooting up he would kick my ass. When I asked Stu why he was threatening me, he said that he considered it his responsibility to look out for me due to our fathers' relationship. Stu went on to explain that he had been shooting up for a couple of years and that it was not something he wanted for me. He explained how he would cycle through shooting, popping, snorting and smoking in order to not compound the consequences of his using. Stu made using needles seem so complicated and unappealing that, more than getting my ass beat, it convinced me not to go that route. I further believe that being a lone wolf user kept me isolated from the temptation of needle use.

So in 1987 I stopped using. I thought Spirit would heal me. It did, physically. The other parts of me were a disaster. All the anger and rage that I used to get away from by getting loaded came back with a vengeance. I really feel sorry for Teri, I was out of my mind and was not as yet capable of containing my emotions. I had more encounters with the police during my early clean time than I had during the entire length of my using.

Fortunately for me, but not for Teri, domestic violence wasn't the hot button issue it was to become later on. In the tradition of my father, getting angry and violent within the confines of one's own home was, by my best thinking, acceptable. This happened multiple times a week. At least once a week, either because of a neighbor or Teri's call, the police would show up at our door. Instead of hauling me off to jail, the police would take me outside and walk me around the block telling me to cool down and get some help with my anger. I would agree but never take any action in that direction and by the next week the episode was repeating itself.

My battle with anger lasted for years. I believe it was only because of the spiritual work I did in conjunction with my Twelve Step work that allowed me to overcome the programming I was infected with. The more I prayed, the more my spirit's vibration was raised closer to the Divine Vibration. The closer I came, the easier it was for me to feel the ego-based shift towards rage and bring it under control. When I added meditation to my regular practices it became easier to recognize and intercede on my anger. After some years of meditation I started to realize that I was no longer reacting to incidents that used to rile me. I believe that regular meditation is the gateway to healing, be it mental, emotional or physical. There is a belief that appears in several esoteric practices, Kabbalah to name one, that states prayer brings God down to humans while meditation raises humans up to God. This has certainly been my experience.

GOD'S IN CHARGE

GOD'S IN CHARGE, IF WE SURRENDER

There are so many instances beyond that which I've already shared that show that Divine Providence is always active in our lives. In fact, I believe that the final lesson of the Second Step is that God, not ourselves, is the ultimate power in our lives. As this subtitle qualifies it, we must surrender. What we must surrender is our ego. That doesn't mean that ego doesn't continue to speak, it means we stop acting on what ego is attempting to mislead us with. Don't allow yourself to become lulled into a false sense of security, as long as we are alive so is ego. Richard Bach said it beautifully in Illusions, page 159; "Here is a test to find whether your mission on earth is finished. If you're alive, it isn't."

This concept of Ego being with us as long as we are alive is best exemplified by the statements attributed to Jesus during the crucifixion. In the Gospel According to Saint Mark, the *King James Version*, Chapter 15, Verse 34:

> "And at the ninth hour Jesus cried with a loud
> voice, saying, Eloi, Eloi, lama sabachthani?"

which is, being interpreted as, My God, my God, why hast thou forsaken me?" In the Gospel According to Saint Luke, the *King James Version*, Chapter 23, Verse 34:

> "Then said Jesus, Father, forgive them;
> for they know not what they do."

Are these two statements a prime example of Ego and Spirit at work in our lives?

In the Gospel of Philip, as translated from the *The Gospel of Philip: Jesus, Mary Magdalene, and the Gnosis of Sacred Union* by Jean-Yves Leloup, page 58, plate 104, logion 21 reads as follows:

> "Those who say that the Lord first died, and then was resurrected, are wrong; for he was first resurrected, and then died. If someone has not first been resurrected, they can only die. If they have already been resurrected, they are alive, as God is Alive."

What if what Philip is referring to is the final transcendence of Ego (the Gospel According to Mark, the *King James Version*, Chapter 15, Verse 34) by Spirit (the Gospel According to Luke, the *King James Version*, Chapter 23, Verse 34)? Maybe, just maybe, Ego was designed perfectly, by a perfect entity, to bring us to this place of ultimate surrender where we no longer see ourselves as separate from each other but one with each other. Or as scripture says in the Gospel According to Saint Matthew, the *King James Version*, Chapter 25, Verse 40:

> "And the King shall answer and say unto them, Verily I say unto you, Inasmuch as ye have done it unto one of the least of these my brethren, ye have done it unto me."

There is another story about Jesus that I want to relate here. In the Gospel According to Saint Luke, the *King James Version*, starting with Chapter 4, Verse 1, Jesus spends forty days and forty nights in the wilderness being tempted by Satan. In ancient Aramaic Satan means adversary. What if the battle Jesus is engaged in is with his Ego and not something or someone outside of himself? At the end of the story Jesus gives Satan a very specific instruction. Jesus doesn't say "you are defeated and will be left here in the wilderness." Jesus doesn't say, "You are defeated and will be shipped to a foreign land." Jesus doesn't say, "You are defeated and will be converted." What was said, as recorded in the Gospel According to Saint Luke, the *King James Version*, Chapter 4, Verse 8:

> "And Jesus answered and said unto him, Get thee behind me, Satan: for it is written, Thou shalt worship the Lord thy God, and him only shalt thou serve."

In the vernacular of Jesus' time, "get thee behind me" is the instruction a master gives to a servant. Maybe Jesus is teaching us that our Ego (Satan, the adversary) is always going to be with us and our job is to become its master?

There is a similar story told about Buddha. It can be found in the *Dhammapada* (which roughly translates to "the path of dharma" [dharma translates to "the way"]) as translated by Eknath Easwaran. The story, in its entirety, can be found, starting on page 38 and finishing on page 41. My interpretation of the story is that it is about Mara, the tempter, (couldn't that be another way of describing ego?) tempting Siddhartha as Siddhartha emerges from the first of what are to become the four sequential Nirvana (the blowing out of all attachment) meditations. With each temptation Siddhartha proceeds to go deeper in meditation. The fourth and final meditation produces the state of Nirvana. Even at this point Mara doesn't stop taunting, what has now emerged as, the Buddha (The Awakened One). The final taunt leads Buddha to make the decision to teach what he has learned.

If Satan and Mara are, as I believe, allegorical tales meant to describe and teach us about our relationship to Ego, then, having now read about these tales, can we be more aware as to what voice we are listening to and acting out behind? Can we be gentle with ourselves when we realize we have been duped by Ego, now knowing the trials both Jesus and Buddha went through in their advanced state?

The following story is another of my experiences where I had to allow Spirit to guide me past my Ego driven fear. I put this story here not to place me at the same table as Jesus and Buddha but to give you, the reader, a more human persona to relate to.

It was the early part of the year 2000 and I had been unemployed for a number of months and my unemployment insurance was soon running out. I had been attempting to find employment but had been unsuccessful. I was at home contemplating my future when the telephone rang. I answered it to find my friend and fellow Twelve Stepper, Susan, on the other end. My first response after the usual greetings and asking how she was, was asking her if she were calling to get back on the radio with me.

You see Susan had been my guest for my second set of shows. My first set of five shows were co-hosted by Tom C. This was done so that I would have a professional, friendly face in the studio with me. As our shows were winding down, Tom instructed me to get a guest who I knew and was comfortable with. Susan immediately came to mind. She had a powerful recovery story which she attributed to her surrender to Spirit.

Susan agreed to do a series of four shows. Our first show would be Susan sharing her recovery story, with the emphasis on Spirit's role in her process. The next three shows were going to be, in sequence, about Steps One, Two and Three. We agreed to take a break after the show on Step Three with the intention of going back on the air at some later date to cover the remaining Steps. Periodically, when I would see Susan at a meeting I would ask her if she was ready to get back in the studio. Susan's answer, in true New Mexican fashion, was mañana. So, naturally, when I heard Susan's voice at the other end of the telephone I assumed that she was calling to discuss getting back on the air. That couldn't have been further from the truth. As time would reveal, Susan and I never did another show.

Susan was calling to tell me that there was a position for a milieu management person at the adult substance abuse treatment center she was counseling at. Susan knew about my prior experience working as a counselor at an adolescent substance abuse treatment center as well as being familiar with my Twelve Step recovery. She had recommended me to the powers that be and was instructed to reach out to me to see if I was interested.

Being in need of work and income I agreed to interview for the position. When I arrived at the treatment center I was directed to the interviewer's office. The first office I passed belonged to an individual

I knew from the Twelve Step rooms, named Juan. When Juan saw me he jumped out of his chair, came to me, shook my hand and welcomed me on-board. Had the decision to hire me already been made? When I arrived at the interviewer's office it was occupied by another of my Twelve Step buddies, Bryan. As it turned out Bryan was the counselor supervisor, and hiring staff was one of his responsibilities.

After a short discussion Bryan made me an offer for a part-time position, three eight-hour shifts. I accepted. Before I could start I needed to obtain a background check and take a TB test. Based on the assumption that I would pass both requirements, Bryan set me up to start my first shift on a Saturday, about a week from our meeting. The Friday night before I started I was doing the household finances. Based upon the hours I was going to be working, at the rate I was going to be paid and adding that to Lin's income, I determined that we weren't going to have enough money to cover the bills. My immediate response was one of fear, that we weren't going have enough money. No sooner had I given energy, fear, to that thought, than a voice in my head said, "Trust God, you will be taken care of." No sooner had the voice spoken than I was calm and at peace and knew everything would be okay.

The next morning I reported to work for my first shift which was to be a training shift. My trainer was Donald, another person I knew from my Twelve Step participation. As we went about my training Donald mentioned to me that he had four shifts a week, three of them with me and one with another staff person. Donald went on to share that he was leaving after this week and that I should ask for the shift that Donald and I didn't share. Shortly thereafter Bryan showed up to do some paper work. I approached Bryan and requested Donald's fourth shift. Bryan had no problem with that and told me that the shift was mine. Bryan then went on to say that the agency policy was that any staff person working 32 or more hours was mandated to attend weekly treatment team meetings, and that since the treatment team meeting took place on a day I was not scheduled to work I would be paid for the time, which usually was four hours. In the space of a few hours I went from twenty-four hours of work to thirty-six hours. There was no doubt God had kept its Word, I was taken care of.

A few weeks went by and I'm again working on the household finances. Again, I multiplied the hours I was going to be working times the rate I was going to be paid, and after adding that to Lin's income I determined that we weren't going to have enough money to pay all of our bills. As before, my first response was one of fear. We weren't going have enough money. What were we going to do? No sooner had I voiced that fear then the same voice as last time spoke to me, saying, "Trust God, you will be taken care of." No sooner had the voice spoken, than a calmness and a peacefulness came over me and I knew everything would be alright.

The next day as I entered the treatment center for my shift I encountered Juan. Juan informed me that he was resigning and that I should apply for his position. Juan ran an extended care program which allowed a handful of clients who graduated from the basic treatment recovery program an opportunity to go out during the day to work and attend Twelve Step meetings, while having a safe place to return to for the evening. I went to see Bryan in his office and informed him that I was interested in filling Juan's vacated position. Bryan's response was that he was going to talk to me about being Juan's replacement, and since we were both in agreement, the position was mine. Bryan went on to inform me that the job was a forty-hour a week job that would require occasional overtime, and that since I was now going to be a counselor as opposed to milieu manager, I would be getting what amounted to be a twenty-percent pay increase. Again, God had kept its word, I was taken care of. As if God ever reneges on its Word.

The surrender of Ego is our ongoing lesson. It's why this dimension of existence was created by the Creator. I could have chosen, because I have Free Will, to stay in or return to fear after God informed me that I would be taken care of. Had I done that, I believe the events as they unfolded would have been different than the way I experienced them. Ego blocks God's Grace and the abundance that comes with that Grace ceases to be presented. I share this lesson with you in the hope that it may help you to avoid blocking your own Grace.

God's In Charge, Even If We Don't Surrender

This section is about the saying "God will do for us what we can't do for ourselves but won't do for us what we can do for ourselves." It was the spring of 1979. I had been working coming up on ten years for a Fortune 500 company. I had started working for them as a purchasing department clerk when they were located in midtown Manhattan. A few years prior to this episode the company decided to relocate their administrative functions to South Brunswick, New Jersey. The thinking was that the corporation would save a lot of money moving the administrative functions to a less expensive rent district and that this move would work because administration didn't require upper management to oversee its functioning. By the time of this move I was a Senior Purchasing Agent.

After a few years the company decided that it was a bad idea moving the administrative functions away from executive management supervision so they were going to move us back to the office building in midtown. I had a really difficult time making the decision to move to New Jersey but I had finally decided to move when they made me an offer I couldn't refuse.

You see, my life was going to radically change. The only decision I had was which aspect of my life would change. I had to choose between losing my job and keeping my residence, or keeping my job and losing my residence. I might have been able to keep both but that would have required me to lose my life as I knew it because I would have to do a brutal, dual direction commute, five days per week, to accomplish this outcome.

So I hemmed and I hawed. One week I was moving, the next week I wasn't. Every time I decided not to move the incentive to move was sweetened. This went on for several weeks. I wish I could tell you that I was actually manipulating the situation but that would not be the truth. I was truly torn and that must have been obvious to the powers that be because they were willing to keep sweetening the pot to keep me. First they offered me a significantly bigger raise. The next time they offered more relocation money, money to cover my traveling back and forth from the Bronx to look for a place to live, as well as first and last month's rent plus the security deposit when I found a place. The next time they offered full coverage of moving expenses including packing and unpacking services. The final incentive was to give me a two year old, low mileage sales fleet car. With that final offer I was told that a commitment from me, one way or another, was needed. I committed to the move. I must have been really valuable to the company for them to go to these lengths to keep me. Can you imagine how valuable I would have been if I wasn't an addict in active addiction?

My first year in New Jersey I would regularly travel back and forth to New York City to socialize and score. Eventually I connected with both local people and dealers, and rarely went back to the city. By the time the company decided to move admin back to New York City I was firmly entrenched. New Jersey was my home. No indecision, no negotiating.

The company's move back to Manhattan was a financial windfall for me. I would be receiving one week severance pay for each of the ten years I was employed, unused vacation and sick leave pay, plus a generous bonus to stay until the move happened and for training my replacement. And on top of that, I was eligible for maximum unemployment benefits because the move was greater than fifty miles. The company moved back to New York City right before the Memorial Day holiday weekend. My best estimate at that time, based upon my recent spending patterns, was that I would have enough money to last me until at least Thanksgiving; if I was really frugal, to New Year's, before I needed to get a job.

How wrong I was. I was about to enter what I call my "wild period." Being an active drug addict and having a wild period almost sounds incongruous, but it was real. The following is not to endorse and/or glorify but to try to impart the craziness that led to God doing for me what I couldn't do for myself.

The group Heart recorded a song titled "Nothing At All." There's a line in that song that goes,

Any thought of moderation would soon disappear.

That best describes the summer of 1979. I didn't have to work, I was single, I had plenty of money and there was nothing I wouldn't try at least once if not twice. There wasn't a party, a score, a sex partner I said no to. On top of all that debauchery, a significant portion of my money was spent on a two-week jaunt (I wasn't working so the term vacation does not seem appropriate) to London and Paris. We, my travel buddy Mary and I, returned from Europe near the end of August. I approached the Labor Day weekend with just enough money to pay my September rent. I was unsure about how I was going to feed myself and keep myself in drugs, since unemployment was a nice supplement but not sufficient enough to keep me in the lifestyle I had become accustomed to. Call it the high cost of low living.

Earlier I mentioned meeting my second wife, Teri, at a party given by Alice, a friend of a sex buddy. That sex buddy was Julie. The group the Eagles recorded a song titled, "Take It Easy." In that song there is a lyric that best describes my life at that time and my relationship with Julie. The lyric is:

"I've got seven women on my mind,
four that want to own me,
two that want to stone me,
one says she's a friend of mine."

Julie was the one saying she's a friend of mine while standing on the cusp of wanting to own me. For a friend she had no apparent problem with having sex with me, anytime, anywhere. We once had sex in the middle of the Princeton University campus. There was this metal sculpture on the grounds of the campus that was shaped like a nut, not the edible kind but the nut and bolt kind, and was large enough for me to sit on and in, and for Julie to sit on my lap. Julie was wearing this long, loose skirt which was easily lifted up when she sat in my lap, and was used to cover how she was really sitting on me and what we were doing. I tell you this and the following in order to paint you a picture of one of the many crazy relationships that populated my summer. In retrospect, how could I not draw crazy relationships to me? I was crazy, my life was crazy. There was an episode, a little bit further down the road after Teri and I hooked up where we invited Julie and Alice over for dinner at Teri's place, which was, by then, my defacto residence. Upon inspection of the chicken Teri had prepared for dinner Julie lit into Teri that the chicken was under-cooked and that I, and not the other guests in attendance, was being put at risk of getting trichinosis. Julie was part sex buddy, part protective Jewish mother, part wannabe lover and part friend. I don't believe those relationships were ever, at any given time, in the same proportion to the other components. Talk about uncertainty.

We'll come back to Julie in a little bit and then the above paragraph will have more meaning. But first there is some more background information that is needed. One of my favorite pastimes during the summer of '79 was to hang out at the local strip clubs. They were supposed to be Go-Go bars but the local law didn't enforce that regulation. Sex, drugs and rock n' roll is a recipe not a sequence. It became a recipe that defined my existence that summer. These bars were the perfect place for me to pass the time of day and night. Occasionally I would score and get to "date" a dancer. There were lots of dancers available because Atlantic City was just starting to be developed with casinos, and dancers were coming from all over the country to be ready when the city took off like an east coast Las Vegas and their particular skill set would be in demand.

It was at one of these bars that I met Carol. Carol was the contractee that ran the kitchen at this particular bar, and she filled the roles of waitress, cook, busser and dish washer. The food wasn't too bad, and there was a connection between Carol and myself. Whenever she had some free time during working hours or after the kitchen closed we would drink and chat together. In a short period of time Carol and I became sex buddies. This added to the incentive to frequent the bar as opposed to, say, hanging out by the pool in the apartment complex I was living in.

Not that sex buddies weren't available at the pool, they were. I was like the rooster guarding the hen house that summer. So many available women and so few, if any, men around. During that summer my sex buddies ranged in age from as young as eighteen, (the daughter of one of my few running partners and if he would have found out he probably would have killed me), to as old as forty-one. I didn't discriminate due to age, race or any other factor. I was an equal opportunity slut.

The pool was good to me, hook-up wise, but the bar was my kind of environment and so that was where I spent the bulk of my time. Spending so much time at the bars afforded me the opportunity to hang out with more and more dancers. So when I returned from Europe unemployed and almost broke, and begin again to revisit my environment of choice, I was inspired to become a go-go dancer. Dancers made good money and the work appealed to me. I would be able to partake in my three favorite pastimes; sex, drugs and rock n' roll, as my vocation and my lifestyle all rolled into one. How efficient is that? I would have women watching me, wanting me, bedding me. Dancers drank for free and nobody paid attention to whatever else you were consuming as long as you didn't get too sloppy. And, I got to choose the music I would dance to.

Timing is everything. That summer was the perfect time to become a male dancer in central New Jersey. Monday Night Football had started airing at the beginning of the decade and had rapidly become an institution. The bar owners realized that Monday had become their worst financial night of the week. That realization led to their next realization, that there was a large, untapped Monday night audience, the wives and girlfriends of those stay-at-home male football watchers, looking for some entertainment. So Monday night became Ladies Night Out at most of these bars. In order to attract this demographic, male dancers and inexpensive drinks were being featured. The successfulness of Monday night Ladies Night led to adding, for some of the bars, an additional Ladies Night during the week. In central New Jersey there was a demand for male dancers that exceeded the supply. In order for me to earn a living that would continue to support me in the lifestyle I had become accustomed to, I would have to work a circuit that covered a much larger territory than just the county I played in. It was a sacrifice I was willing to make.

Earlier in this book I discussed an experience I had at a Club Med. That experience wasn't the only significant one I had there. It was just the only spiritual one. The remainder of those experiences were hedonistic in nature. The one that ties into this story has to do with the color war activity that the club conducted the next to last day of my stay there. The activity was a competition where the entire club population was divided into four camps, each one flying a different colored flag. The final contest of the competition was an evening talent show that each color group was to perform for the remainder of the camp. One of the members of my group was a high school music teacher and dance choreographer. She took charge of this activity, devising a presentation that mimicked the musical "South Pacific." The way she explained it, there would be a chorus line, a group of lip syncing singers and a featured dancer who would do a lower torso/hip gyration as part of the finale. For the main dancer she wanted a male. All the males in hearing range of this description either walked away or bowed their head in hope of not being chosen. For whatever reason I gave the gyration a try. The teacher saw me and immediately designated me as the one.

By the time of the finale all four groups were so close together point wise, that the winner of the talent competition would also be the winner of the color war. I started the performance dressed as a member of the chorus line. I was wearing a white dress shirt and a pair of navy blue shorts. Close to the end of the performance two of the lip syncing singers picked up a strategically placed blanket and held it up like a screen. I stepped out from my position on the chorus line to stand behind the blanket. I whipped off my shirt and tossed it aside like a professional stripper. The blanket was dropped and there I stood with a painted torso and chest. There was a rippling water line painted across my belly button extending out in both directions with a boat floating in the middle of the water. Each of my nipples had a seagull painted above them. The audience roared in appreciation and an exhibitionist was born.

My color group won the talent contest hands down and therefore the overall competition. I can't remember if there was a prize for winning the competition, but if there was, it would have paled to the personal rewards I received. I became a club celebrity. More women than I could count offered to buy me drinks. Some even offered me their bodies. The woman who got to take me "home" for the night was the one with the best pickup line. She asked me, "Can you move horizontally like you did on stage, vertically?"

Having the Club Med experience imprinted in my memory banks made the decision to become a go-go dancer a no brainer. I created several tapes to dance to and started dancing in front of a mirror, working on my moves, my facial expressions and my tease. I danced for a couple of hours a day. Back in those days you didn't need a ripped body to be a dancer. Based upon the numerous hours I spent at the bars and the conversations I had with the dancers, the ones who made the most money and had the largest followings were the ones who could connect with their audience. I also, through a dancer-supplied connection, ordered some costumes to dance in.

With everything in or near being in place I set up my audition. There was a bar a mile or so from my apartment that was having an open audition a week from the coming Monday night. Mary, my European traveling companion, was the main bartender at that bar. She made arrangements with the owner to insure I would be able to audition. I was on my way.

The Tuesday prior to my audition I hooked up with Julie. When I explained my situation to Julie she offered to help me get a job. You see, Julie was the owner of an employment agency. During our discussion Julie informed me that a position at my level, both responsibility and salary wise, would probably take at least six to eight weeks to secure. I agreed to allow Julie to represent me even though my plan was to become a dancer.

There's a saying in Twelve Step that goes, "You want to make God laugh, tell God your plans." The Thursday after meeting with Julie I came home to a message from Julie. She had secured me an interview as a Director of Purchasing for a proprietary drug company for the following day. I agreed to go on the interview. After the interview I called Julie and asked her if she received any feedback regarding the interview. Julie advised me that the owner of the company was impressed with the interview. Early Monday morning Julie called to tell me that they really wanted me and wanted to offer me the job at a salary that was more than the range we had originally discussed. Because the money was so outrageous and because Julie would receive a huge recruiting bonus I agreed to take the job.

I titled this section "God's In Charge, Even If We Don't Surrender" and stated that it is about the saying "God will do for us what we can't do for ourselves but won't do for us what we can do for ourselves." With the hindsight brought on by years of intending and practicing, to the best of my ability, Yogi Bhajan's basic teaching (more shall be revealed in the final chapter) I can say, unequivocally, that the hand of The Divine was ever present in the events described above. God knew that my becoming a dancer was a train wreck waiting to happen. This is not an indictment of go-go dancers or strippers, it's an honest evaluation of myself and my motivations at that particular time in my life. I have no doubt that my best thinking would have brought about my demise. Whether I would have died from an overdose, or a drug related death, or from a sexually transmitted disease or at the hands of an irate husband who caught me with his wife, I would not have survived the experience I chose to inflict upon myself. Death was inevitable. God did for me what I couldn't do for myself: save my sorry ass from what seemed like the most perfect career move I could possibly make.

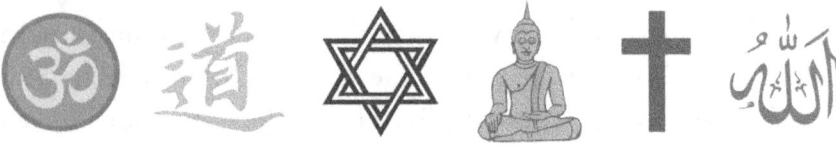

MAULANA ZAINULABEDIN-KAZMI IS

Of all my teachers in the physical, the teacher who has advanced me the furthest, and who had the greatest impact on my soul, was Maulana Zainulabedin-Kazmi.

Listen to Sufi Saint Maulana Zainulabedin-Kazmi's teachings on what constitutes True Spirituality. You will hear in Maulana's own words his 10 insights on True Spirituality. The written copy can be found in the section "Maulana on Charity," that begins on page 96 at the bottom of the first paragraph, as well as the entire section, "Maulana on True Spirituality," starting on page 98.

This book features the cutting-edge Augmented Reality technology of RealityX2. Just download the free RealityX2 App from the Apple App

Store or from Google Play to experience the enhanced content that is intended to enrich your reading experience and expand your understanding of God and the Spiritual realm.

INSTRUCTIONS
1. Download the free App for iOS or Android
2. Open the App on your Smartphone or Tablet
3. Point your camera at the image above this copy
4. Enjoy!

What follows is some of our walk together. It was early December, 2000 and I'd been on the air about 18 months when I first heard of Maulana. This came about as a result of my constant searching through the classified sections of the local newspapers. I was committed to the spiritual diversification of my radio show. Living in Santa Fe, New Mexico was a big plus, allowing me access to a broad spectrum of spiritual teachers that regularly came to Santa Fe to instruct. The advanced event notifications and contact information were easily found in the bulletin board section of the classified ads. As a regular reader I noticed recurring announcements citing a restaurant south of town, The Whispering Dove, that was consistently hosting visiting Sufi masters. I called the number and wound up speaking with Alima, the owner of the restaurant. I introduced myself to Alima, explaining to her about my radio show and my search for guests. Alima told me that she had been a practicing Sufi for over 20 years and that her restaurant had become a regular meeting place for the various visiting Sufi masters passing through the southwest. I asked if it would be possible to get one of these masters to be a guest on my show. Alima promised to inquire on my behalf of her upcoming visitors and get back to me.

A couple of weeks later I received the promised phone call from Alima. She informed that there was a powerful master, whose title was Maulana, which means Saint, coming to Santa Fe in January and that he agreed to be a guest on my show. Still being somewhat of a radio novice and therefore a bit overly cautious I already had guests booked into February. I asked Alima if it would be alright to record the shows for future airing. Alima said she would check and get back with me. The following day Alima called and told me that prerecording the show was acceptable. I made arrangements with the production team at the radio station, booking the studio and an engineer for a maximum of four thirty-minute prerecords and then confirmed the day and time with Alima. I was excited and nervous. I was excited because of the stature of my guest and I was nervous because this was going to be the first show I would do without previously communicating with the guest.

Maulana and his entourage, which consisted of Sajeedah, his wife, his oldest son Atif, and Alima arrived at the station exactly on time. Because of the tight production schedule there was little time for getting acquainted. I started to get spooked when Maulana was first introduced to me, he had such a heavy accent, an accent I was to later learn was a combination of Indian, Pakistani and British. There were some awkward first minutes during the interview but as the conversation progressed I started to get a handle on Maulana's accent and speech pattern. You see his speech pattern consisted of answers to my questions, pauses of varying degrees of short lengths, and then further answering of the questions.

We recorded four half-hour shows, each one following the train of thought started in the previous show. Maulana, revealed after the fact, that he was given free rein to answer all of my questions without censor. The two recorded hours are so chock full of so much amazing spiritual information that, if I were to attempt to cover it here, it would create a book of its own. The best way to obtain the lessons is to listen to the audio files of the show. They can be found on my website https://churchoftheonegod.org in the table under the subject "Sufism" on the "Words of the Prophets Radio Shows" page within the "Rev. Phil on Mass Media" menu.

As if the interview were not enough, what happened afterwards was even more personally profound. I walked Maulana and his guests to their car. I said my thanks and goodbyes and was about to leave when Maulana told me to wait. He opened the rear door of his SUV revealing numerous bags obviously stuffed with many items. Maulana started handing me items from the bags. I received a picture of Mecca, a picture of Medina, a sheet of paper with Sufi prayers on one side and a trio of pictures on the other side. The pictures were of Maulana, Maulana's Master and Maulana's Master's Master. I was given a few pictures of Maulana, some hard sucking candies and what I was told was a taweez. The taweez was a talisman made by Maulana's students. It consisted of a folded triangular piece of leather that encompassed a prayer on a piece of paper. The leather was stitched around the prayer and a string that was used to tie it around one's neck. The finished taweez was then brought to a Zikr presided over by Maulana, where it was blessed. The blessing given it provided the wearer with protection and health. I have worn a taweez ever since, taking it off only when showering.

As the television commercial would say, "But wait, there's more." Maulana called over Sajeedah and started handing her bags from the SUV. Maulana dug out a bag from the drivers seat side of the storage area and handed me a prayer cap and a prayer jacket. As Maulana was handing these to me I could feel the startled reaction of Alima, who was standing by my side. I was so taken with the gifts, especially the final two, that all I could do was express my thanks and gratitude. Maulana repacked the SUV and everyone piled in and they left. I was totally confused by what had just transpired.

First thing the next morning I called Alima to see if she could shed some light on what had transpired the day before. More specifically, what was the meaning of the prayer cap and prayer jacket. I felt like I had been adopted. Alima stated that she had never seen the gifting of the cap and jacket before and didn't have any idea as to their meaning or even if there was a meaning. I asked Alima if Maulana was around. Alima informed that the family hit the road at sun up. I asked her if they were going to return to Santa Fe any time soon. Alima told me that Maulana entered the U.S. on a 90-day travel visa, that his visit to Santa Fe was very near the end of his journey and that he would have to return to London for 90 days before he could obtain another travel visa. It appeared I would have to wait five or six months before I could ask all the questions that were adding up in my head.

Maulana And My Heart

It was a Friday in the middle of March, a couple of months had passed, when I receive a telephone call from Alima. She called to inform me that Maulana was back in Santa Fe. Alima explained that the family had returned in order to arrange a marriage between Atif and the daughter of a prominent Sufi family in Santa Fe. I asked Alima if Maulana was staying with her this time around. Alima informed me that the family was staying with their future in-laws. Alima went on to state that whenever Maulana was in Santa Fe, he regularly made an appearance at Tribes, a downtown Santa Fe coffee shop, at noon. Maulana did this in order to be available for anyone who wanted to ask him a question or receive a blessing.

As I had stated earlier I was, and still am, an active member of a Twelve Step fellowship. The morning I received Alima's call was the morning of the start of that fellowship's yearly statewide convention. Due to a shortage of funds I hadn't planned on attending. I had a goodly amount of free time on my hands before the potential noon appearance of Maulana. Since all my fellowship friends were either at or on their way to the convention, I was at a loss as to how to keep myself amused.

Aloud, I asked the question, "What should I do?" This voice in my head said, fairly forcefully, "Go to the radio station." Knowing how to take direction I drove to the radio station. When I arrived at the station it was operating on automation due to building construction.

Again, aloud, I asked the question, "What should I do now?." Again, by a forceful voice, I was told, "Go to the cafeteria." So I proceeded to go to the cafeteria. Once there, I looked around and spotted Tom C., the station Program Director. I joined him at his table and we sat and chatted for a couple of hours. At a little past eleven I told Tom that Maulana was back in Santa Fe and that there was a good chance that he would make an appearance at noon at Tribes.

Tom had engineered the interviews with Maulana and had met briefly with Maulana afterward, so he was aware of what a gift it was getting to meet with Maulana in an intimate setting. Little did either of us know what a gift we were about to receive.

As we were leaving the cafeteria Tom suggested it would be easier to park only one vehicle downtown, that we should drop my car off back at my house and take his car to Tribes. I found this a little unusual but nevertheless agreed. The significance of this offer didn't become clear until later. In a day of Divine Guidance and Synchronicities this gesture got right in line.

We arrived downtown and immediately found a parking spot directly across the street from Tribes. It was almost noon when we entered Tribes, finding the shop empty. I asked the individual behind the counter if Maulana was coming today and the attendant stated that he was running a little late but would be arriving soon. Tom and I took seats at a big round table. Soon thereafter Maulana and his entourage arrived. Maulana sat to my left and the rest of his party, his wife, his son and Alima sat to the right of Tom, who was on my immediate right. The rest of the shop, except for the barrister, was empty.

I turned to Maulana and said "I have some questions for you." Maulana's response was "I know." I asked my first question, "When you gave me the prayer jacket and cap was I being adopted?" Maulana answered "No" and proceeded to explain why he gave me those items. Maulana explained that he was in constant contact with his Master and was instructed to give me these items by his Master. During his answer, at a point where I thought he might be finished speaking, I turned towards Tom to share what I had just heard. At that point Maulana grabbed hold of my shirt sleeve and gently tugged me back towards him. He then proceeded to talk some more, answering my questions, some of which I hadn't asked. There were a couple more instances where I thought Maulana was done and turned to Tom to share all the amazing things Maulana had shared with me. Each time I did Maulana would grab me by my shirt sleeve and pull me back. What I thought would be the last time Maulana would pull me back, he went on to share that when he paused he was checking in with his Master, who he was in constant connection with. Maulana told me I was asking questions that required his Master's approval for Maulana to answer. This time I was sure Maulana was finished, so again I turned to Tom only to feel Maulana gently tugging me back to him. Before I knew it Maulana was placing the first finger of his right hand on the upper left-hand side of my heart. As soon as Maulana's finger touched my heart I was transported to another time and place, I know not where. I'm not sure how long I was gone for, either. What I do know was related to me by Tom. At some point Tom felt something energetic, looked over at Maulana and myself and realized what was happening. At that point Tom took hold of my right hand and placed it on his heart. Tom then proceeded to place his right hand on the heart of the person to his right, who mimicked his action with the person to their right. This action was continued until there was a daisy chain emanating from Maulana through my heart and down my right arm until everyone seated at the table was connected.

At some point Maulana was finished with my energetic transfusion, removed his finger from my heart, stood up and proceeded to leave. I was physically speechless. I also felt a disconnect from my being. I'm not sure how long I sat there in a daze. When I was able to stand up Maulana and his party were gone. Tom and I went to his car and he drove me home. Taking Tom's car was an act of Divine intervention. I was so high I would not have been able to navigate my way home without having an accident.

I stayed euphoric the remainder of the day. When I awoke the following morning, Saturday, I decided I was going to go to the convention. I was still in an altered state but felt in touch enough with my being to be able to drive to Albuquerque. When I arrived at the convention everyone I ran into who knew me asked me if I had relapsed. Obviously my altered state was apparent to everyone. The altered state lasted through to Monday. When I woke up Monday I could tell I was pretty much back to normal, whatever that meant as applied to myself. I do want to state at this point that the high

I experienced from Maulana far and away exceeded any high I had ever achieved from drugs.

As spectacular as the short term effects of what Maulana had done to me were, the long term effects were way more significant. What I experienced was a huge reduction, almost an elimination, of my anger. I had been programmed to respond with anger to almost any adverse situation. Throughout my early recovery I had been focusing on dealing with my anger. I worked both a first and a Fourth Step focusing on anger. In one fell swoop Maulana practically eliminated it. Prior to this experience I was working hard to not act out my anger. Afterwards I was hardly responding in anger much less needing to control my emotional demonstration. Basically I became more accepting of life on life's terms and, therefore, more serene.

Maulana identified himself as a Naqshbandi Sufi. As he explained it, the Naqshbandi school of belief was all about a clean heart. As Maulana described it, "Naqshbandi means to imprint, to engrave, to stamp the name of God onto the heart." One of Maulana's most frequent teachings was that "Heavenly knowledges are poured into the heart" and "God says I cannot come between earth and sky but I can come into a clean heart." The only conclusion I can come to is that Maulana cleaned out my heart. Let me expound on this last statement a little bit. I don't believe that my physical heart was the sole recipient of this cleansing. We are, at our core, spiritual beings. Our bodies feel pain and that pain is conducted to our spirit. This is how the physical teaches the spiritual. So when I say that my heart was cleansed I'm referring to my spiritual heart, my heart chakra. Maulana, in his own way, eradicated a lot of my karma. What makes this even more interesting is that Maulana, because of his learnings and his self-realization, didn't believe in chakras or karma.

The place where Maulana touched my heart stayed sensitive for a couple of years. I could always, first time, every time, touch the exact spot where Maulana did his work. It always felt different than any other area surrounding my physical heart. Two years passed before I was able to be with Maulana again. It was during that time, at a

GOD IS

Zikr, that I asked Maulana for a blessing. Maulana placed his hands on my head and blessed me. The energy I felt during this blessing was strong but soothing. I didn't notice right away, which is not to say that it didn't happen instantaneously, that my sensitivity at Maulana's place of touch was gone. I can still go straight to the spot Maulana touched but it no longer is sensitive.

Maulana And My Master

During the radio interview I did with Maulana in January, 2004 the subject of my having a Master came up (Maulana and I recorded two 60-minute radio shows, which can be found on my website https://churchoftheonegod.org in the table under the Subject: "Sufism", Prophetic Topic: "I Can Come Into A Clean Heart," parts one and two on the "Words of the Prophets Radio Shows" page within the "Rev. Phil on Mass Media" menu). The shows discussions were an extension of the original four shows I did with Maulana back in 2001. Because of the strong connection I felt with Maulana I asked Maulana if he was to become my Master. I had been operating, up until that point, behind the belief that my path was to be a non-affiliated one, that I was walking a spiritual, not a religious path and that being a representative of a religion would, at the very least, hinder the message I was here to deliver if not eradicate it entirely. The idea of becoming a Sufi was as disconcerting as the idea of becoming a practitioner of any religion. The concept went against what I had learned as a Twelve Stepper, that I am a spiritual being not a religious being. However, the idea of having a Master, a teacher (read sponsor) was at the very heart of the Twelve Step program. I was, at the very least, torn and confused. Maulana quickly resolved my conflict by stating that he was not to become my Master, he was going to be the conduit for it. I was relieved but still confused. I asked Maulana what he meant by the word conduit. Maulana's response was not very helpful. He restated the phrase by defining conduit but not explaining how it was going to come about. I asked Maulana what I was supposed to do and he responded with the direction that I pray daily for a Master to be presented to me and that one would be.

For the next two or so years, as part of my morning regimen, I thanked Spirit for providing me with a Master (I had learned, somewhere on my path, that I'm not supposed to ask God for anything because my asking would imply that I knew better than God what I needed. The appropriate prayer is one of thankfulness and gratitude). Throughout the remainder of each day I stayed vigilant in my awareness as to who was being presented to me. I was blessed, during those two plus years, to meet a number of likely Master candidates. I met them, like Maulana, through the vehicle of my radio show. Each time a potential candidate was presented I did a God check. The check consisted of asking the question "God, is this the One?" Each time my Spirit, my intuitive sense, my gut, however you want to label it, told me no. Each time I was both disappointed and relieved. I was disappointed because I had come to believe that I really needed a Master to guide me to the next levels, whatever those were. I was relieved because, like Maulana, each of the potential Masters, was affiliated with a religion. After a couple possibilities leading to a no response I started to doubt if there were ever going to be someone sufficiently advanced and non-affiliated to become my Master. Nevertheless, I continued, daily, with my morning thankfulness prayer and my daily vigilance.

When Maulana returned to Santa Fe I sat down with him and had a discussion mostly concerning my Master. I was impatient; I could hardly wait for the niceties and catching up to end. As soon as I sensed an opening I jumped in, feet first. I told Maulana that I had followed his directions and had prayed for a Master to be presented and that, as far as I could determine, none had been presented. Maulana gave me a huge smile and asked me why did I believe my prayers weren't answered. My response was, "because there is no one I am working with." I went on to review the possibilities that were presented to me and the God checks that told me no. Maulana smiled again and said, "Do you remember me telling you that I would be the conduit for your Master?" I responded "yes." "Well I didn't say that without meaning" was Maulana's response. I basically responded "okay." Maulana went on to explain that God was aware of who I was and what I needed, and that a human Master wasn't going to work for me and the mission I had. What Maulana stated next floored me. He stated that through his request and God's response, I was given a Spirit Master and that the Spirit Master had been with me from the moment of my first prayer of thankfulness for one.

As soon as Maulana explained this to me I had a revelation. At that time, January, 2004, I had been working as a counselor at a substance abuse/mental health treatment center. I didn't recall the precise date that it started but I remembered having insights, in sessions with clients, where I would answer questions and/or make statements that I knew were accurate while having no idea how I knew or where I had learned the information from. I also started choosing, from several different analogies to get a point across, what seemed to the client as the example that the client especially related to. I never put this upgrade in my communication skills together with the concept that I was being fed insights and information by a Spirit Master. The analogy aspect I wrote off to an ever-increasing gift of empathy that I believed I possessed. The origin of the new information was another matter. I had no answer as to what its source was and, after a while of getting no insights, I just accepted it as it was and didn't give it any more thought. I am pleased to report that my Spirit Master must still be with me because the demonstrations stated above are still manifesting in my life.

There is so much more that I learned from Maulana that I could write about here but won't write about all of them. I would suggest that if you want to learn more of Maulana's teachings there are four hours of interviews on my web site, address previously given, that you can listen to.

MAULANA ON CHARITY

There are, however, a few lessons that Maulana taught that I would like to write about. The first has to do with giving charity. This lesson was a private lesson, a discussion on the radio and a teaching at a Zikr. Maulana's teaching was that it is better to do daily charity, in smaller amounts, then sitting down once in a while and writing a large check. The daily practice gifts us with the constant reminder of God and, therefore, the reminder of being of service. Selfless service to others is the ultimate demonstration of our spiritual practice and growth. Maulana teaches, "In true spirituality servitude is a very high station because servitude makes you to be humble. No one can enter into the Divine Presence with pride. The only way you can enter is when you are humble. Humble comes with servitude."

What Lin and I do, per Maulana's instructions, is every morning when able, we sit at the edge of our bed and I hold Lin's hand that is holding the box we put our donation in. We place a dollar in the box and then, silently, each of us says our own prayer. My prayer is as follows: "In the name of God, in the name of Mercy, we make our daily charitable contribution. God, thank you for the abundance in our lives and thank you God for the spiritual guidance that shows us how to share that abundance with others."

On the first of each month we take the previous month's donation, place it in a baggie and alternate carrying it with us until we are presented with someone or some cause to give it to. Giving the money away is accompanied by the simple statement, "With God's Grace."

I can't begin to describe how good the giving away of the donation feels. Writing a check, no matter the size, never approaches the heartwarming feeling that giving away that baggie does.

Maulana On Mercy

Maulana always starts his teachings with the statement "**GOD IS** most Gracious, most Merciful. If anybody wants to be Gracious, has to be Merciful." Maulana would also state that "Mercy is a very high attribute and name of God. Mercy is the biggest ocean and the very high attribute of God and Allah. Everything else: love, compassion, kindness are drops into the ocean of mercy." Maulana would go on to teach that "Mercy is like an ocean in Paradise, millions times bigger than this planet of earth." I remember Maulana, during one of our private sessions stating, "In the Koran there are mentioned 99 Attributes of God. Of those 99 attributes Mercy is one of the highest." This confused me. I asked Maulana if Mercy was greater than Love, greater than Compassion. Maulana's response was that Love and Compassion were based on choices, a connection with another human being. Mercy had no such attachment. That love and compassion doesn't apply to everyone but mercy does. What I've come to believe is that Maulana's use of the term Mercy equals my use of the term Unconditional Love.

I will close this section with my favorite Maulana description of God's Mercy. "Take one step to God walking and God will take ten steps to you running."

Maulana On True Spirituality

During the four hours of radio interviews I did with Maulana, Maulana defined true spirituality in a variety of statements. Some of these statements were:

"In true spirituality any knowledge which makes a person to be proud one is a useless knowledge. Any knowledge which makes a person to be humble is a good knowledge."

"True spirituality progresses and proceeds in the dark."

"In true spirituality time and space have no meaning."

"In true spirituality that where there is the end and the extinct of all energy there is the starting of true spirituality."

"In true spirituality there is no holy book, there is no revelation, there is no command of God. That God has ever said I can come into the brain of a scholar, or a lecturer or an engineer or a professor or a doctor or a scientist or a prime minister or a president or a king or a queen, there isn't any. God says I cannot come between earth and sky but I can come into a clean heart."

"In true spirituality there are stations. There are no senior and junior. There are stations which God can give to whoever he likes."

"A true saint who working for the will of God in true spirituality can be in seventy places at the same time. As more and more servitude being carried out and that person can be in more and more places."

"In true spirituality there is no third eye, fourth ear, fifth arm or sixth leg. There are two eyes and two ears in the heart. That is how a true master, a true saint can see people."

"In true spirituality there is no coincident, no accident, it is all arranged."

Each of the statements above, on their own, I believe, gives us an unprecedented insiders' view of the spiritual realm. As a collection of statements this section acts as a guidebook, teaching us about our relationship to the Divine Providence, our fellow spiritual beings and our ego. These statements are even more powerful when placed in the context of the teachings of the Maulana, as heard on the radio shows. If any of these statements touches your heart then give yourself a gift and listen to the radio shows, in their entirety, at the website listed earlier. Your Soul will be illuminated and your Spirit will shine. I know that my journey has been made all that much easier and sweeter because of Maulana's teachings.

MARK AND THE RADIO

I see all of our human experience as a result of karma bringing us to crossroads and then our choosing either Divine Will or Self-Will as our guide. I connected with only one individual during my 26 years of addiction who still remains in my life today. That individual is Mark Scali.

This is not to say that I was always as close to Mark as I am today. I wasn't. Yet we always managed to stay in touch even if years passed between our contacts. One of those extended times and the ensuing reconnection set the tone and course for my life as it is today. It's because of Mark that I became a host of a spiritual talk radio show which led to my hosting a spiritual talk television show which has placed me in a position to launch a spiritually-based radio station.

I have, over the course of my broadcast career, met some incredibly spiritual individuals and because of my discussions with them I have grown in spirit beyond my ability to quantify. Obviously, God's Will prevailed at the crossroads I am about to relate.

During the early part of 1996 my wife to be, Lin, and I had just started our second extended road trip in four years. We were spending the winter in Savannah, GA. I was inspired to call my old friend, Mark, who I hadn't talked to in probably a couple of years. During the conversation Mark told me that he had a dream in which I was interviewing him on a radio show. I had been aware for a long time that Mark had precognitive dreams that were extremely accurate, however, this dream I had a hard time believing in.

Lin and I returned to Santa Fe, New Mexico around Christmas of 1996, as husband and wife. I obtained a job almost immediately upon my return, as a counselor in a long-term adolescent treatment center. Troubles involving my work situation began when managed care came to New Mexico in the early part of 1997. By this time Mark and I had not only reconnected, our friendship had grown to a whole new level. This led me to contact Mark, to get his input on what he thought I should do. The outcome of that conversation was instrumental in my becoming an Ordained Minister and founding Church of the One God.

I received my ordination on September 15, 1997. On August 27, 1998, Church of the One God met the requirements for obtaining tax-exempt status, 501(c)(3), from the Internal Revenue Service. Once Church of the One God was recognized by the IRS, I went about creating a website. The purpose of the website was to carry a message of hope, that by working and walking a spiritual program, any individual could change their life significantly for the better.

In early February, 1999, the conversation I had with Mark three years earlier returned to mind. The web site had been completed and launched and I was wondering what to do next. As with times in the past, I asked what should I do now? That voice of Spirit reminded me of that phone conversation. I realized that a radio show would be an excellent vehicle to carry the Creator's message of hope. I contacted the local community public radio station, KSFR, 90.7 FM, and proposed to the program director, Tom C., a show based upon my website. Tom guided me in translating my website into a format that would work on the radio.

The fruits of that effort became my first radio show, "Good Company." "Good Company" was a 30-minute talk show that aired on Saturday afternoons. It aired weekly from June 5, 1999 until August 25, 2001. After a brief hiatus, I returned to the radio air waves on October 17, 2001 with "Words of the Prophets," a 60-minute talk show that encouraged listener participation. Since its inception "Words of the Prophets" experienced several time slot changes. The stated purpose for both "Good Company" and "Words of the Prophets" was:

- To introduce the listening audience to as many as possible of the wide variety of religious and spiritual paths that are available to them.
- To familiarize the listening audience to the guiding principles that are taught by each of those paths.
- To discuss how the listening audience can put into practice, in all phases of their daily lives, the principles espoused by those paths.

The transition from radio to television is another one of those Divinely Synchronized events that I will discuss later on. There are, however, some First Cause coordinated events that merit sharing here.

MY RADIO DHARMA

God, September 11, 2001 and My Radio Dharma

I awoke, pretty much like everyone else in the Mountain Time Zone, to the news that the World Trade Center buildings in New York City were destroyed by terrorists who flew airplanes into them. I watched the news for hours, which may have been the last time I ever gave that much attention to any news event. I called Lin to find out if she heard from her youngest daughter, Andrea, who went to school across the street from the towers. Lin was unable to reach her until later in the day when the phone lines were a little less in use. It turned out that Andrea over slept and didn't make it to school that morning. The statistic I remember is that the fatality level, between the airplanes and building occupancy was around one third of the amount it could have been. For me that screams of an unconditionally loving deity intervening in the lives of thousands upon thousands of individuals and their families.

The above is just the background, not the point, for this segment of this narrative. There is some more background information that I must impart to you before I get to the story behind this chapter's title. First is that during my prior radio days I had, on occasion, done what I called special event shows. These were shows that looked at a current event from a spiritual perspective. For these special shows I would recruit Tom C., the program director, to co-host with me. We did shows on the Columbine, CO school massacre, the fire that destroyed a significant portion of Los Alamos, NM and a shooting on the Santa Fe, NM Plaza during Fiesta.

I used the term prior in the above paragraph because at the time of September 11th I was no longer on the air. I was working as a counselor at a residential treatment center as a substance abuse intern and was preparing to test for my full license. Around the beginning of August, 2001, I received a letter informing me that the licensing board had voted to raise the minimum standards needed to qualify for the test. Reviewing the new standards revealed to me that I would need to go back to school in order to qualify to take the test. Working a full time job didn't afford me much time for school and homework. At the time I was doing my weekly spiritual talk show "Good Company" which was on air for thirty minutes, plus I was DJing a weekly two hour on air rock and roll show called "Night Journey." The prep time required to produce these two shows came to about twice the air time. All totaled, I was committing approximately seven and one-half hours to my radio endeavors. I had to make a decision as to where my greatest good was situated. "Good Company" was a worthy endeavor, however, "Night Journey" was nothing more than a childhood fantasy being fulfilled. Because I was an all-or-nothing kind of guy back then, I decided to walk away from both shows. My greatest good appeared to be as a counselor. I saw this block of time as something that needed to be cut in order to have enough time for my school work. I gave Tom notice on both of my shows. By September 1, 2001 I would no longer be on the air. No sooner did I give Tom notice then the time slots got filled. Shortly thereafter I received another notice in the mail stating that the licensing board had decided to grandfather in all interns who met the then testing requirements. Talk about a mixed reaction. I was elated that I didn't have to go back to school and I was sad over the fact that I was no longer on the air.

Wednesday, September 12th, early AM, I called Tom and left him a message stating that I wanted to do a Special on the events of the previous day. I knew he would know what I meant. A couple of hours later I received a phone call from a guy named Bob. Bob explained that he hosted a weekly, hour long, environmental show every Wednesday evening. He wanted to do a show on the events of the previous day but didn't feel like he could do the show by himself. He called Tom, requesting help in locating a co-host. Tom, having heard my message, gave Bob my phone number and suggested that he call me. Bob and I discussed what he wanted to do with his show and we were in agreement that we wanted to look at cause, effect, and what could be done, from a spiritual perspective, to prevent the events of the previous day from being repeated in the future.

Bob and I did the show that night and from my perspective we carried a powerful message that was well received. The show was everything I had wanted "Good Company" to be. It was sixty minutes as opposed to the thirty I had. It was a weekday night not an early Saturday afternoon. The day and time slot was significant because the listening audience would more than likely be home and able to call in as opposed to the slot I had wherein the audience would be listening from their car and, therefore, less likely to call in. That night we had seven call-ins. I know that the events of the previous day was a major factor in the audience participation, but still, I would probably have to do two months' worth of shows to get seven call-ins.

I awoke the next morning and as I did almost every morning, I immediately engaged in my meditative practice. This meditation started very differently from my usual meditative endeavors. My mind didn't resist, it didn't take me on a road trip of irrelevant, unwanted sites. I was in a rarely reached space of total surrender of self, both mind and body. I'm not sure how long I was in that state when a booming voice spoke to me. It had a message I'll never forget. The message was "Radio is part of your path, do not forsake it." I believe this was The Creator speaking to me. Why do I believe this? Because never in my life, prior or since, have I used the word "forsake."

As soon as the Voice was finished speaking my meditation ended. I immediately picked up the phone, called Tom and left him a message requesting that we meet. A little while later Tom called me back and we set up a breakfast meeting for the following morning at the college cafeteria.

Over breakfast I shared with Tom my impressions of the show I did with Bob, the experience I had during the previous day's meditation and my request to be placed on the wait list for a weekday night, sixty-minute time slot. Tom told me that Bob had stated that a weekly show was too much for him and that Bob might be receptive to alternating weekly broadcasts. It was here that Tom and I miscommunicated. I thought Tom was going to contact Bob while Tom thought I was going to contact Bob.

A couple of weeks had passed and I hadn't heard from Tom or Bob. I called Tom and set up a breakfast for the following morning, which was a Wednesday. Over breakfast I asked Tom what was happening with the alternating weekly show. It was then that our miscommunication was revealed. Tom thought we had left it that I was going to call Bob while I was under the impression that Tom was going to make the call. We finished breakfast and went back to Tom's office. Tom had one of those phones that had clear buttons that would light up to show incoming calls or a phone in use. There was also a red button that flashed when there was a message. When we arrived at Tom's office his red button was flashing. Tom listened to his message and when it was finished he turned to me smiling. Tom shared that the message was from Bob, that Bob had just, effective immediately, surrendered his time slot, that there wasn't enough time in Bob's life for him to continue doing the show. Tom asked me if I wanted the slot. Of course I said yes. Tom then asked me if I could be on the air that night. I laughed and told Tom that he trained me too well, that you don't throw a brand new show together in a few hours, that I would be ready to air in two weeks. Tom was alright with that, and that was the birth of "Words of the Prophets."

Spirit wasn't fooling around when it told me, "Radio is part of your path, do not forsake it." Spirit wanted me on the air and Spirit made it so. I know that some of you reading this will call this sequence of events coincidence. By itself, without the rest of this narrative, that might be plausible. However, in the context of all else that has been written here, can that concept really stand up?

My Radio Dharma, The Next Phase: Television

I was let go by KSFR; my last show aired on May 31, 2008. I saw this as Divine Intervention. God was doing for me what I couldn't do for myself, removing from my plate what was, at the time, my least important endeavor. At the time I was working full time in private practice as a spiritual counselor, as well as producing both a play about substance addiction recovery, and an all-day recovery from substance addiction celebration, both for the Santa Fe Recovery Center. I was a member of the board of directors and like in the army if you had an idea and wanted to see it made so, you were told to do it. I was volunteered. My spiritual growth was such at the time that I knew these two events were being presented to me for the greater good and it wasn't my place to refuse to take on the tasks. Both the play and the celebration were fund and consciousness raisers. I had some helpers but the two productions were eating up large chunks of my time. I believed in the message given to me on September 13th so I saw being let go by the radio station as a temporary relief effort.

One of the intentions for the play was to have it videoed so that DVDs could be produced for sale and given as gifts to donors. When I first started on radio the Santa Fe Community College had a media department that encompassed both the radio and television stations. A few years down the road, for financial reasons, the two entities were split apart, becoming standalone operations. During the time of the combined department, regular staff meetings were held, and attendance was mandatory for both media disciplines. Due to the meetings I learned that the television Operations Manager, Doreen, had a private video production company. When it came time to contract for the videoing of the play I reached out to Doreen. We were quickly able to come to terms for the complete package.

GOD IS

The play had its run in late September. By the middle of October Doreen and I started the video reviewing process as the precursor to the editing process. Due to the holiday season the editing process extended until the early spring. During the editing Doreen half asked, half stated that I was no longer on the radio. I affirmed. Doreen then asked me if I would be interested in producing/hosting a television show. I told Doreen I would pray about it and get back with her. My prayer requesting to be shown where my greatest good would be made manifest produced a resounding yes response to doing the television show.

Before finalizing the production agreement I communicated with Doreen via email, inquiring as to certain aspects of the contractual arrangement. There were about a dozen points I requested clarification on. When I received Doreen's response I knew that television was where I was supposed to be. All of Doreen's answers were the responses I felt were necessary for me to move forward. "Words of the Prophets," the television version, was born on June 9, 2009.

My Radio Dharma, The Ongoing Saga: A Radio Station

The television show lasted approximately four and a half years. Due to a variety of factors the number of original shows I was doing dropped from about thirty something shows per year to about half that amount. I was finding it increasingly more difficult to schedule the programming I felt was consistent with the message I believed I was meant to carry. I came to believe that I should be back on the radio, that radio would afford me the access and flexibility I believed I needed.

It was early winter, 2012 and by this time the General Manager who had let me go from KSFR was no longer on staff at the station. I decided to draft a show proposal letter to the station and emailed it. I believed I was both remembered and well-liked by the existing management of the radio station and that they might be receptive to the idea of my returning to do a weekly spiritual talk show. Time passed and I didn't receive a response to my email.

Even though the television and radio stations were split apart years before, they still occupied the same physical space, sharing the same access and corridor. The station's engineer James and assistant engineer Wendy, who were both connected to the radio station when I was last with it, shared an office down the hall from the entrance to the television broadcast studio.

One day, a few months after I submitted my show proposal, while out at the television station for who knows what, I showed up at James and Wendy's office door, to find only Wendy at work that day. We chatted for a while and then I asked Wendy if she knew anything about my proposal, if any decision had been made with regards to it. Wendy informed me that no decision could possibly have been made since there was no one designated to make that type of decision. Wendy went on to explain that a committee was being formed to evaluate new program proposals and that she was on that committee. From our discussion I found out that there were a number of available time slots and I allowed myself to believe that I would be one of the chosen new programs.

Overlapping the above, I had been in a discussion with a woman, Barbara, who had been a guest on both my radio and television shows. She wanted to start a blog radio show and wanted me to co-host with her. I discussed with Barbara a trial run to determine if we had the chemistry necessary to do a regular radio show.

Just as we were getting ready to do the trial I put a hold on it, believing that I would be, shortly, doing a regular show on KSFR. The KSFR option was far and away my primary choice. No sooner did I put the trial on hold then KSFR fired their General Manager and by doing so put a hold on any new programming. Instead of going forward with the blog radio I decided in fairness to Barbara that I would wait a little while to allow KSFR to do a new hire and see if mine was still a suitable show for them.

A couple of months later, with no forward movement on the hire of a new General Manager, I was out at the college campus taking care of some television business first and then running an errand for my sister at the college bookstore, which was in a different building from the television station. I finished my television business and headed across the courtyard to the bookstore building. I was turning the corner where the cafeteria was when I practically body slammed another individual. Lo and behold the person I had nearly trampled was Donna, my first engineer when I started doing radio. I hadn't seen Donna in at least half a decade, if not longer. Neither of us had time to catch up so we exchanged cards promising to reach out to each other shortly.

I forget who made the call but the call was made and Donna and I met for breakfast within a week. Over breakfast, we filled in the other about where we had been, what we had done and our best thinking regarding the future. Donna shared that she had run a public radio station in the state of Washington and was now working as an independent consultant, assisting radio stations start-up. I shared that I was strongly leaning towards walking away from the television show and was looking to get back on the radio – either a land-based station and/or an Internet station.

It was at this juncture in our conversation that Donna mentioned that the FCC was getting ready to release eight low power FM signals in Santa Fe. I questioned what a low power signal was and what it would take to be awarded a signal. As Donna explained the qualifying requirements and the process, I could feel Divine Synchronicity at work in my life, one more time. To further demonstrate the concept of Divine Synchronicity, Donna and I shared a similar vision of the message that the radio station should carry, a holistic, diverse spiritual, social justice lineup of programs.

As it turned out I had the organization, Church of the One God, that could qualify under FCC guidelines, as well as the connections in both the spiritual and social justice realms to provide the bulk of the programming the station would need to meet FCC requirements. Donna had the knowledge, both from a FCC standpoint as well as a technical aspect to build, launch and sustain a radio station.

Donna and I agreed to be partners. We, with the support of the Church of the One God Board of Directors, complied with all the FCC requirements and filed our application accurately and on time. On February 12, 2014 Church of the One God was awarded a construction permit for the Santa Fe, New Mexico Low Power FM signal 105.5. The call letters chosen were KVTP, the K being mandated by the FCC, the VTP chosen for the phrase "Voice of The People."

When God told me, back on September 13, 2001, that radio was part of my path, little did I know that meant starting up and running a spiritual radio station. In retrospect I can see that everything I experienced in the 15 years of being in broadcast media is invaluable to the tasks that are being presented to Donna and me today, and I am sure, those that have yet to come. What I have come to believe is that The Creator will always present me with my greatest good. It's up to me to get my ego out of the way and allow it to unfold the way an entity beyond my comprehension has laid it out. Faith leads to trust, trust leads to acceptance, and acceptance leads to serenity.

EMANUEL SWEDENBORG, EDGAR CAYCE, VAISHALI, LINDA DRAKE AND ME

I have been blessed with many gifts as a result of being the producer and host of a spiritual talk show on both radio and television. The gifts always begin with the individuals I get to meet and they then grow to the discussions we have regarding the infinite aspects of Spirit. Every now and then one of these individuals has a destiny to be more than just an interview. The show was the vehicle to connect us with each other. Maulana is a prime example of this dynamic. Another such example is Vaishali.

I was first introduced to Vaishali (her name was given her by one of her teachers and is the name of a small town in India that was frequently visited by the Buddha) in the early part of 2007. I was contacted by her public relations representatives who were headquartered in Albuquerque. Vaishali was soon coming to Santa Fe to do a book signing as a part of her tour in support of her self-published first book *You Are What You Love*. *You Are What You Love* is a modernized, plain language rendering synopsizing the writings and the teachings of the mystic Emanuel Swedenborg.

Emanuel Swedenborg was born in Sweden in January, 1688 and died in March, 1772. Swedenborg was a scientist, philosopher, theologian and a mystic. It is told that Swedenborg mastered every known physical science of his day. Swedenborg claimed he did this in order to discover where the Soul resided. As the story goes, at the age of fifty-seven Swedenborg was visited by an angel and was told that all levels of the spiritual realm were now open to him, that he now could travel back and forth between earth and the spirit realm at will. For the remaining twenty-seven years of his life he did so, taking copious notes that he then published as books. These books, in a modern language translation series, are available through the Swedenborg Foundation. For a more in-depth accounting of Swedenborg's life, including some of his so called minor miracles, you can listen to my radio show interviews with both Vaishali and/ or Rev. Grant Schnarr of the Swedenborg inspired "New Church." They can be found on my website https://churchoftheonegod.org in the table under the Subject: "Emanuel Swedenborg" on the "Words of the Prophets Radio Shows" page within the "Rev. Phil on Mass Media" menu. There is also a two part audio file of the lecture

GOD IS

Vaishali gave at the Association for Research and Enlightenment (the organization whose primary function is to house and disseminate the information found in the transcripts of Edgar Cayce's psychic readings) about Emanuel Swedenborg that can be found on my web site https://churchoftheonegod.org on the "Like Mind/Like Kind" page.

Vaishali and I hit it off from the very first moment we met. It was obvious that we had both originated from the same family group of the same Soul collective. Vaishali, when I first met her, was running a book publishing company, Purple Haze Press, in addition to hosting two radio shows, one from a California land based station and one from an Internet radio station, as well as being a lecturer and teacher, being certified as a natural health practitioner of Chi Nei Tsang, an internal organ massage therapy and a student of Ayurveda. In addition to being a guest on my radio shows Vaishali also guested on a few of my television shows can be found on my website https://churchoftheonegod.org on the "Words of the Prophets Television Shows" page within the "Rev. Phil on Mass Media" menu, and through her many contacts provided me with a handful of wonderful guests.

There were numerous times during our communications that Vaishali and I engaged in a dialog whose topic can be best and most easily summed up as "my mystic is better than your mystic." During one of these debates I mentioned to Vaishali that I felt I had a very powerful connection to Edgar Cayce, that I must have, in a previous life, walked with the spirit that was Edgar Cayce. Vaishali's response really surprised me. She asked me, "Would you like to find out?" My response was "of course" followed by "how." Vaishali told me about a recent guest she had on her radio show named Linda Drake.

Linda was a channel for Abraham. Abraham, as Linda describes them, are a group consciousness of high vibrational spiritual beings whose purpose is to bring humanity the wisdom and guidance of God for the advancement of their soul's journey. Abraham became known in the 1980's, being channeled by Esther Hicks and her husband Jerry, writing books based on the channeled information of Abraham. As Vaishali explained it, Abraham would be able to access my past lives and would be able to tell me if my intuitive sense was accurate or not. Vaishali went on to tell me that Linda had written an Abraham channeled book about death and grief entitled *Reaching Through the Veil to Heal*. Vaishali provided me with contact information for Linda and gave me permission to use her name as a reference.

I reached out to Linda, via email, and we set a date, November 17, 2007, to do a live telephone interview radio show. The show, which wound up in three parts, can be found on my website https://churchoftheonegod.org in the table under the Subject: "Death and Grief" on the "Words of the Prophets Radio Shows" page within the "Rev. Phil on Mass Media" menu. By this time my show was 30 minutes in length and I was my own engineer. The show that preceded mine was always prerecorded, so as the incoming engineer it was my job to end the previous show, play the scheduled underwriting and public service announcements and start my own show. Normally I would arrive 10 or so minutes before my show was supposed to start to get the transition organized. For the Linda interview I showed up a half hour early since I had scheduled a pre-air conversation with Linda so that we could acquaint ourselves with each other and discuss what we hoped to cover during the broadcast.

During our get acquainted conversation I shared with Linda the exchange with Vaishali that was the impetus for my conversation with Linda and the subsequent show. When Linda heard this tale her response was, "Do you want me to ask Abraham for you?" I was hesitant. I didn't want to make the show about me. Doing that, according to the training I received from Tom C, was ego based, bad radio. However, I was so intrigued by the question and even more so by whatever the answer would be that I couldn't just say no. The compromise I reached with myself was that we would proceed following the outline for the show that Linda and I constructed via email and if the opportunity and/or the time presented itself, I would bring up the subject.

Interviewing Linda was a unique encounter. When I interviewed Maulana, his pauses to check in with his Master as to what he was allowed to share with me and the audience was a fascinating dynamic. Linda's interview was even more unique. Maulana's communications with his Master were silent. With Linda I would ask a question and she would relay it to Abraham, Abraham would communicate with Linda in a way that only she could hear, and she would either repeat the response over the air or enter into a further dialogue with Abraham. The best way I can describe what it sounded like was listening in on only one end of a conference call, not hearing the conference attendees just the conference leader, knowing from the questioning that you were able to hear that several responders were talking at the same time and that Linda was attempting to manage the multiple replies in order to achieve a cohesive response.

Towards the end of the show, with maybe seven or so minutes remaining, Linda and I had covered the outlined points satisfactorily and Linda had agreed to do at least one more on air interview. Instead of improvising and opening up a topic that we couldn't do justice to I indicated to Linda that I wanted to change direction and ask Abraham the Edgar Cayce question. The way I phrased the question was, "Is there a place in time where I was walking with the same spirit that became Edgar Cayce?"

Abraham's response (the ensuing dialogue, can be heard, in its entirety, on my website https://churchoftheonegod.org in the audio file "Edgar Cayce & Rev. Phil - Part 1", on the "Like Mind/Like Kind" page), was, "Yes, you had a very strong connection with Edgar Cayce, and that's why, when you read his information on his writings you know it's truth because you know you were there in his lifetime, you were there as a part of his life." Another piece of information passed on by Abraham was that, "You were there for part of his writings, assisting him with it, but none of your information was written in his books."

That last piece of information from Abraham was interesting, in retrospect, since Edgar Cayce never really wrote anything himself. All of the information attributed to Edgar Cayce came through him while he was in a trance state, channeling what was referred to as the source. I was so blown away by what I was hearing that I was more focused on what was being said and what was to come, as opposed to the content of the statement. This is not to say that that last statement invalidates what came before it or what came after it. I, for the sake of perspective, needed to share this. Channeling, like any communication, can be tricky. My questions may be misleading or not in the proper context. What Abraham might be saying and how Linda is passing it on may be somewhat different. Semantics, as it usually does, may play a big part in the conflicting statement. It's up to you, the reader, to draw your own conclusions. As they say in those television only offerings, "But wait, there's more."

After a series of related comments between Linda and myself I asked Linda "Was there other lifetimes I walked with the spirit that was Edgar Cayce?" Through Linda Abraham answered, "Yes, that's why the two of you were so strong in that lifetime when he was Edgar Cayce. They're saying yes, you had four previous lives before the one where his name was Edgar Cayce. So the two of you were very, very strong energies together."

The following day I received an email from a psychic who lived in a small town south of Santa Fe named Madrid. The psychic stated that she had listened to the show and found it very interesting. She shared that she had spent a year living in Virginia Beach, Virginia, the location of the A.R.E., spending the majority of her time at the A.R.E. attending lectures, taking classes and reading the Cayce readings. She went on to state that she was intrigued by the reading I received from Abraham and, when she had time, she checked the Abraham reading with her own spirit sources and they confirmed the accuracy of the reading. She went on to say that the attachments to the email she had sent contained information about the people who were in Cayce's inner circle and that I was one of them. The psychic either couldn't or wouldn't identify the individual. She instructed me to pray for the answer to be revealed and that I would intuit who I had been during that time with Edgar Cayce. I followed her instructions and received a gut level response to my prayer. The response I got was the name Arthur Lammers. Arthur Lammers was credited with a major turning point in the readings. In 1923 Arthur requested a reading on astrology. In the reading the concept of reincarnation was mentioned. This question started a whole new type of reading. Up to that point the requests for readings were about health related issues. The new category, past life readings, became a major focus of future readings.

The concept that I was, in this walk with Edgar Cayce, Arthur Lammers was cast doubt upon when Vaishali shared a channeled reading she had obtained from a psychic named Johane Rutledge. Johane was a guest on one of Vaishali's radio shows. Johane claimed to channel Edgar Cayce. During the interview Vaishali asked the channeled Edgar Cayce about his relationship with the spirit who is currently Rev. Phil. This segment of Vaishali's interview with Johane can be heard on my website https://churchoftheonegod.org in the audio file "Edgar Cayce & Rev. Phil - Part 2", on the "Like Mind/Like Kind" page

Johane/Edgar stated during a response to a question by Vaishali that the spirit that was Edgar Cayce and the spirit that is currently Rev. Phil were boyhood friends, best friends, during Edgar's childhood and were in a Catholic choir together. This statement is in contradiction to the known facts of Edgar Cayce's childhood. He was born a Protestant, and remained one throughout his entire life, belonging to the Disciples of Christ church.

Contradictions abound in the interpretations of spirit-originated psychic readings. I believe that there are a number of factors that contribute to the diversity of information on any particular subject. The level of skill of the channel is paramount. Not all channels are tapping into the same source. Some channel their higher self. Some channel a spirit on a lower plane, say a level five. Some channel a spirit on a higher plane, say a level seven. The source of the information then gets filtered through the channel. This is impacted by the channel's ability to interpret what is being given.

An example that might clarify the above explanation is an individual attempting to explain to a child a difficult aspect of astrophysics, such as the forming and properties of a black hole. If the source of the explanation is a Nobel Prize winning astrophysicist and the interpreter is a trained early education teacher and the child has a rudimentary understanding of the subject, the outcome will be at a higher cognitive level than if the source of the explanation is a lab technician, the interpreter has no early education training and the child having an attention deficit disorder. This example is representative of only one of the multiple variables that could impact a reading.

Despite the contradictions presented regarding my relationship with the spirit that was Edgar Cayce my intuitive sense tells me that there was a relationship between the two of us. There are too many converging factors, a preponderance of evidence, that for me, override the inconsistencies presented in the various psychic readings. Of course there is the potential for a certain amount of ego boosting that accompanies this gut feeling but not enough to negate the feeling. Could this book that you are reading be the master stroke of this life's karmic blueprint? As the Grateful Dead once said in "Box of Rain",

If you need it believe it, if not pass it on.

A DEMONSTRATION OF UNCONDITIONAL LOVE: A SOUL MATE FOR ALL TIME AND SPACE

On my way to Dulce, the coffee shop I've done a great deal of writing this autobiography at, I had Meat Loaf's *Bat Out of Hell* in my car CD player. In my opinion this CD is one of the all-time greatest. There's nothing but great music on it, none of the seven songs are fluff. The song that came out of the speakers when I pushed the play button, the song that I played over and over again during the drive this morning was "For Crying Out Loud" written by Jim Steinman. The Divine Synchronicity that I am about to start writing this chapter of the book this morning and that this song comes blasting out of the speakers in my Explorer does not escape my notice. I've always related to, and frequently learned from, music lyrics, especially, nowadays, when it comes to songs that express my love for Lin. One of these days I'm going to create a mix CD or two, containing nothing but Lin-inspired songs. The lyrics at the end of "For Crying Out Loud" are worth looking at. They are, starting at the final refrain:

GOD IS

For crying out loud you know I love you
For crying out loud you know I love you
Oh for crying out loud you know I love you
For crying out loud you know I love you

For taking in the rain when I'm feeling so dry
For giving me the answers when I'm asking you why?
And my oh my
For that I thank you

For taking in the sun when I'm feelin' so cold
For giving me a child when my body is old
And don't you know
For that I need you

For coming to my room when you know
I'm alone
For finding me a highway for driving me home
And you gotta know
For that I serve you

For pulling me away when I'm starting to fall
For revvin' me up when I'm starting to stall
And all in all
For that I want you

For taking and for giving
And for playing the game
For praying for my future in the days
that remain
Oh Lord for that I hold you

Ah but most of all for crying out loud
For that I love you
Ah but most of all for crying out loud
For that I love you
Ah but most of all for crying out loud
For that I love you

When you're crying out loud
You know I love you

The Gospel of Rev. Phil

This book is a declaration of my love for God. This chapter is a declaration of my love for my wife, my partner, my soul mate: Lin. Lin has appeared, popped up if you will, in a number of places in this book and to this point I have not really introduced her. Lin and I met in Roselle Park, New Jersey. I was newly clean and had taken a job as a salesperson for a printing company. The company occupied a building across a driveway from its sister company, a typography firm. Lin was a second shift supervisor for the typography company. The first time I met Lin I was taken by her powerful, gentle energy. I know that sounds like a contradiction in terms, but it isn't. Lin's energy out-radiated everyone else's. I constantly looked for excuses to be at the typography company when Lin was working.

I was married to Teri at the time but my fidelity to that relationship was non-existent. The relationship was a battleground and we were constantly in conflict. I saw no hope of salvaging the relationship. Besides, the attraction to Lin was so damn powerful; I was drawn like the proverbial moth to the flame. The more contact I had with Lin the more I wanted. I finally asked Lin out on a date. Our first date was a free radio station concert on the boardwalk in Asbury Park, New

GOD IS

Jersey. It went well enough for the two of us to be willing to continue seeing each other. It didn't take long for us to become lovers.

There are numerous song lyrics that describe how I feel about Lin. The one that stands out most is from Peter Gabriel's "In Your Eyes". The lyrics that best summed up my feelings for Lin are:

> *In your eyes*
> *The light the heat*
> *In your eyes*
> *I am complete*
> *In your eyes*
> *I see the doorway to a thousand churches*
> *In your eyes*
> *The resolution of all the fruitless searches*
> *In your eyes*
> *I see the light and the heat*
> *In your eyes*
> *Oh, I want to be that complete*
> *I want to touch the light*
> *The heat I see in your eyes*

I'll never forget how I loved to kiss Lin's eyes. I was blessed, beyond my ability to recognize, to be connected to Lin. There was no judgment in those eyes or in any other aspect of Lin's persona. Having been perceived as being judged inadequate for my entire life, being with Lin was, as the Eagles sang:

> *A peaceful, easy feeling.*

In spite of these powerful feelings for Lin I was not above almost shattering what was, without a doubt, the most loving, healthy, functional relationship I had ever experienced (the details of which are scattered throughout this autobiography). The reasons Lin and I are still together are attributable to The Great Spirit's patience with me and Lin's ability to love me in spite of my attitudes and actions. Lin understood me as no one else had ever done. There are a couple of stanzas in the Harry Chapin song "Shooting Star" that sum this up best for me. They are:

He was crazy of course
From the first she must have known it
But still she went on with him
And she never once had shown it
And she took him off the street
And she dried his tears of grieving
She listened to his visions
She believed in his believe-ins
    and:
He was dancing to some music
No one else had ever heard
He'd speak in unknown languages
She would translate every word
And then when the world was laughing
At his castles in the sky
She'd hold him in her body
Till he once again could fly

I've been blessed on this journey with some incredible teachers. This book highlights a few of those relationships and the lessons they facilitated. Each one of those teachers taught me, basically, the same lesson: "**GOD IS** Unconditional Love." The teachings' were just that, teachings. They were theory sandwiched between abstract, non-personal experiential interpretation. These teachers were, at best, short term demonstrators of a concept. In order to replicate a life's lesson one needs to, I believe, have that lesson demonstrated sufficiently enough that the individual can reproduce it.

There are three phases to a lesson. The first phase is the acquisition of new information. In this scenario, for me, the new information is that Love doesn't need to be conditional, that Love doesn't have to lead to pain, that Love is not an emotion but is a spiritual demonstration. That in spite of my fear-driven anger, in spite of my selfish, self-centered dysfunctional behavior, in spite of my toxicity, I am Loveable and Loved. My working of Step Two in my Twelve Step work showed me that The Creator loves me unconditionally. But that was God, not another human being.

The second phase is the integration of this new information into my existing body of beliefs. In this case I had to overwrite the belief that I was, ultimately, unlovable, that I was such a broken individual that I would eventually, usually sooner than later, royally screw up the relationship and drive the individual who was loving me away. This was my perception, based upon the repeated experiences in my life. If my father couldn't love me, if my extended family couldn't love me, why would anyone else? If my first and second wives were mirroring back so much pain that I couldn't stand the sight of my reflection, why wouldn't this be repeated again. For this Soul, this integration process required repeated demonstrations, more than I care to attempt to count. I was starting to love myself unconditionally. I was learning to "hate the sin, love the sinner." But that was self-love. Could I be loved unconditionally, or close to unconditionally by another human being? Lin showed me that it was not only possible but doable. In spite of the ways I behaved, the ways I let Ego run, and almost ruin, my life, Lin never stopped loving me. That didn't mean I was lovable. That came with the third phase.

As part of the journey from phase two to phase three, with God's Grace, I eventually taught myself that I was my own worst enemy, my own worst critic. My greatest weapon, my biggest lesson, of choice, was self-sabotage. And through it all, Lin never stopped loving me. I do only a few prayers every morning. I don't believe in prayer much, especially prayers of request. The prayers I do are prayers of intent, thankfulness and gratitude. One of those regular prayers goes as follows: "Thank you God for the presence of Lin in my life, for she is a wonderful demonstrator of the virtues I need to implement and by allowing her to walk this path with me you have made this journey that much easier. Amen."

The third and last phase in the lesson process is the demonstration. Once we have successfully integrated the new information, we will, by Divine Design, be given the opportunity to demonstrate our level of proficiency. In a sense our successful integration can only be determined by our demonstration. The demonstration can, and usually does, take a number of progressive, successive expressions. At some point during this demonstration process the new information for our next lesson is being acquired. Remember Richard Bach's statement from earlier? (No? Then see page 72.)

As Lin continued to demonstrate her near-unconditional Love for me I was able to replicate it towards others. It started with my demonstration towards Lin and has since spread to others in my life. One of the first if not the first, thing I tell my new clients and sponsees is that they can never anger me or disappoint me. I still have a long way to go to be at the level of demonstration that Lin is but I am, I believe, moving forward on this front. I am, beyond my ability to express, eternally grateful for Lin walking this path with me and her showing me how to move beyond the near-impenetrable, protective shell I had placed around myself and allow Love to flow inward and outward.

The title for this chapter uses the phrase "Soul Mate." My use of the term is meant to imply, in the context of the title, a soul that I have spent numerous lifetimes walking and working with. In March, 2008 Lin and I took a road trip to Austin, Texas to visit with our Soul Group brother and sister, Hector and Sharon. Since Linda Drake also lived in Austin we set up an appointment for a psychic reading from Abraham. The reading had a powerful impact on Lin and me, both individually and together. This reading is not posted because unlike all the other readings posted on the Church's web site this reading contains information about individuals other than the two of us, information which we were sure wasn't ours to release to the world.

One aspect of the reading, the one that gave birth to this chapter's title was the answer to a question I asked of Abraham. The question was "How many lives have Lin and Phil walked through together?" Abraham's answer was 32. Abraham went on to explain that the relationships Lin and I shared were varied. Sometimes we were friends, sometimes we were enemies, sometimes we were siblings. There were times we were responsible for the other's death. As Abraham summed it up: "Once you start interacting with another Soul from your Soul Group you'll just keep on coming in. You'll just keep on having that experience with them in some way, swapping genders, swapping types of relationships. You had this swapping back and forth, covering each other's backs, being there for each other, helping each other with your issues. Because you had these issues in many lifetimes, just haven't gotten them all resolved. By this point both of you said: 'Hey, let's do it this way. I know it's going to be hard but we're going to come in with all the issues and we're going to work our way through them.'" So here we both are, working our way through them. I know, without a doubt, that whatever issues don't get resolved this lifetime we will address, as partners, in another lifetime, because Lin and I are "Soul Mates For All Time And Space."

Lin and I did a follow up reading with Abraham, through Linda Drake, in May, 2013. It is in two parts and they both can be heard on my website https://churchoftheonegod.org under the subject "The Soul's Journey: Reincarnation & Karma - Parts 1 & 2" on the "Like Mind/Like Kind" page.

THE GOSPEL OF REV. PHIL

The word "Gospel," as defined by the Merriam-Webster online dictionary, when used as a noun that is not being used as an interpretation of the Christian message, is:
    a. the message or teachings of a religious teacher
    b. something accepted or promoted as infallible truth or as a guiding principle or doctrine.

Dictionary.com defines the non-Christian noun as:
    a. something regarded as true and implicitly believed
    b. a doctrine regarded as of prime importance

The etymology of the word, according to Wikipedia, derives from the Old English gōd-spell, meaning "good news" or "glad tidings."

Over the course of time there have been numerous spiritual texts with the word Gospel in their title, writings that carry an author's belief as to the message or teachings of a religious teacher, and/or something that is being accepted or promoted as infallible truth, or as a guiding principle or doctrine. In reality, for most, if not all, of those books that contain the word Gospel in their title, we have no idea who actually wrote them and how much of the writing really represents the titled source's views, as opposed to the author's interpretation of those teachings. In this category there are the Canonical Gospels: Mark, Matthew, Luke and John. We also have the Jewish-Christian Gospels, the Gnostic Gospels, the Infancy Gospels, the Lost Gospels; as well as numerous other Gospels that fall within such categories as Medieval Gospels, Modern Gospels, Fragmentary Gospels and more.

GOD IS

One of my favorite Gospels is "The Gospel of Sri Ramakrishna" by Mahendranath Gupta.

Based upon the numerous number of texts containing the word Gospel in their title I don't feel that I have crossed some sacred line in using that word in my title. I have Good News to spread. I have the messages or teachings of a religious teacher and/or something accepted or promoted as infallible truth or as a guiding principle or doctrine. I have something regarded as true and implicitly believed and/or a doctrine regarded as being of prime importance.

Let me get clear about this autobiography. The experiences written about are uniquely mine. The lessons I draw from these experiences and the teachings that are birthed there are not mine. They come from the Creator, whether they come through one of my teachers or come through me doesn't mean we created them or possess them. We don't, we are just the channels used to disseminate the information.

Yogi Bhajan, peace be upon him, who was the spiritual leader of Sikh Dharma of the Western Hemisphere, would teach, "If you don't see God in all, you don't see God at all." Everything is God. Everywhere is God. Everyone is God. We are One with God, therefore we are One with Everything, Everywhere and Everyone! Maybe this adds clarity to the statement attributed to Jesus in the Gospel According to Saint Matthew, the *King James Version*, Chapter 25, Verse 40 which reads as follows:

> "And the King shall answer and say unto them, Verily I say unto you, Inasmuch as ye have done it unto one of the least of these my brethren, ye have done it unto me."

Maybe, just maybe, the more we as Spiritual Beings having a Human experience can embrace this realization of oneness, the less damage we will inflict on ourselves and others. In order to achieve this goal we will need tools to aid us on our journey. One of these tools, which was transmitted through me, is a spiritual version of the therapeutic modality called Cognitive Behavioral Therapy. It is called IAI. It is as follows and can, if it serves you better, be downloaded from my website at https://churchoftheonegod.org on the "IAI" page under the "Tools" menu.

IAI

Please note: The use of the terms "Spirit" and "God" in the following paragraphs are not meant to be misconstrued as over-riding your own belief system. The terms are being used generically. Feel free to substitute whatever name, term or phrase resonates with you.

The letters IAI stand for three parts of a process that allows us to change the way our brains react to stimuli. The letters stand for: Intention, Awareness and Intervention. It is strongly recommended that this process becomes incorporated into the practice the reader does the first thing every morning. These three components are specifically designed to achieve two objectives. The first objective is to start the practitioner off on their day centered in their Spirit instead of their Ego. This is based upon the belief that duality exists in each and every one of us. There is a Native American folk tale that best sums up my beliefs. In it a grandfather is lecturing his grandson, telling him that each human being is made up of two wolves, a good wolf and a bad wolf. The grandfather goes on to explain that the two wolves are in constant battle with each other. At this point the grandson asks "Which wolf wins the battle?" The grandfather replies, "Whichever one you feed." I call the good wolf Spirit and the bad wolf Ego. In the Twelve Step community, there is an acronym for Ego that is "Edging God Out." The second objective this practice achieves is to focus the brain, both the cognitive and non-cognitive sections, on new ways of responding instead of old ways of reacting.

Prayer is a very personal practice and differs from one person to another. There is no wrong way to pray. As Rumi once said, "There's a thousand ways to kneel and kiss the ground." What I believe this means is that each and every one of us are one with the Creator. Therefore everything we think, feel, say and do are transmitted instantaneously to the Creator. What distinguishes prayer from other forms of communications is having the intention of wanting the Creator to be addressed.

There is one thing I have learned about praying that I would like to pass on to you. It is that all prayers should be an expression of gratitude and not a request. We should start each of our prayers with a phrase such as "Thank you God for" instead of "God, please give me." The expression of gratitude accomplishes two things. First, it doesn't presume that we know better than God what we need. The second is that it implies a state of abundance as opposed to a condition of lacking. The following are the intentional prayers I recommend saying on a daily basis. I recommend always starting with a prayer that affirms our Divinity. The reason for starting this way is that it immediately lifts us out of our default lower state of existence, Ego, and into our optional higher state of existence, Spirit. The following prayers are being listed as suggestions only. You are a Child of the Creator, create your own or feel free to use mine or some combination thereof.

IAI - THE PRACTICE

Intention:
Our actions create the reality of our lives. There are two powerful tools that we possess that guide our actions: our intentions and our beliefs. There are several ways we can state our intentions. There is prayer, affirmation, contemplation, and just plain conversation. The key to any form of transmission is that it is intended as a message from ourselves to our Higher Power. I recommend always starting with a statement that affirms our Divinity. The reason for starting this way is that we are immediately lifted out of our default lower state of existence, Ego, and into our optional higher state of existence, Spirit. After that I suggest starting with a couple of intentions that are demonstrations of the Divinity that we are acknowledging.

To start with I suggest setting the following four intentions.

1st: Acknowledge your own Divinity, in any way you are comfortable doing so. (Example; I am One with God in Love and Light.)

2nd: Is a demonstration of your Divinity by intending to practice, as best as you can, unconditional love for yourself and others. (Example; Thank you God for showing me how to be unconditionally loving of myself and others.)

3rd: Is a demonstration of your unconditional love by intending to practice, as best as possible, forgiveness for yourself and others. (example: Thank you God for showing me how to be forgiving of myself and others.)

4th: Intend to eliminate a behavior that is interfering with your ability to live a serene and joyous life. (example: Thank you God for removing the obsession and compulsion to act out in anger today.)

This is the minimal practice. Additional spiritual practice after these four intentional prayers is definitely encouraged. Treat your Spirit as a muscle. The more you exercise it the stronger it becomes.

Awareness:

This means, as best as you can throughout your waking hours, being as aware as possible, of your thoughts, feelings and actions. Anytime your awareness shows you that you are going against any of your morning intentions, you go to the third letter, the second "I."

The IAI's awareness component brings an additional blessing. As we raise our awareness during the day we are training ourselves to be more aware during our meditation. When we become more aware in meditation it facilitates our spending more time in quiet then chatter. As we become more aware of chatter in our meditation we are training ourselves to be more self-aware during the day, showing us more quickly when we are not living up to our intentions. The cross pollination will continue to work as long as we are practicing both components.

Intervention:

When you become aware that you are going against your intentions, you need to intervene on yourself. You need to do this gently. If you are not gentle with yourself, not only are you going against your intentions, you are creating an atmosphere that will perpetuate the behavior you want to intervene on. An example of a gentle intervention is, "Stop, this doesn't serve me anymore." After you state your intervention you then repeat the morning intention that you are not complying with until your thought, feeling and/or action is back in compliance with your morning intention. You may find yourself intervening numerous times throughout your day. This is alright. This indicates that you are becoming more aware. The need for intervention has always been there, it's just you were so accepting of the ego chatter you didn't see that it wasn't serving you.

The above description of the IAI is just the starting point, not the entire path. Spiritual practice is not meant to be complex or complicated. Spiritual practice is meant to be simple though it may not always be easy. The simplification of the IAI comes in the Intention and Intervention sections. We can combine the four intentions stated above into one intention, such as this paraphrase of an Emanuel Swedenborg teaching: "My job is to act as if God was supposed to show up but couldn't make it and asked me to take its place." Or as Edgar Cayce said (reading 5392-1, paragraph 8, given August 28, 1944) "Use the power thus generated - not to self-indulgence - but to beautify, but make the world a better place because ye have lived in it."

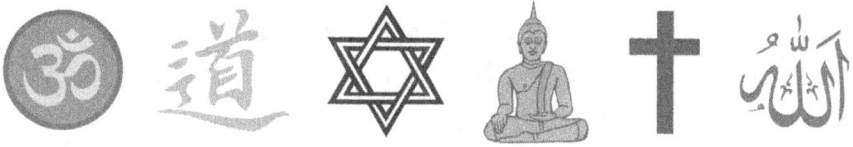

REVELATION

The Gospel of Rev. Phil is that The Creator loves its creations unconditionally. The fact that I am alive and capable of writing this story is proof positive of that statement. In spite of the wreckage I created for myself and inflicted on others, God never judged me, never gave up on me. **GOD IS** non-judgmental. God repeatedly intervened in my life, saving me from myself, in the hope that I would, at the next crossroad, choose to walk towards the light instead of away from it. I didn't need to be a disciple or devotee of any teacher, practice or religion in order for God to provide me with an option of light. **GOD IS** unconditionally loving. I didn't need to address God by a certain name, I just needed to choose whatever I wanted to name this entity, and not self-will, to be my guiding force. I didn't need to meditate or pray in a certain way; I needed to just surrender in whatever fashion resonated with me. I didn't need to prostrate myself in a prescribed fashion, I needed to master my ego. **GOD IS** unconcerned with ceremony, ritual and dogma, just my Soul's development. My being was enough for the option of progressive enlightenment to be offered. I didn't have to save my Soul, I had to educate it.

My repeatedly choosing to walk towards the darkness instead of the light never damned me to hell. Because of the Great Spirit's love for me I was given as many opportunities as I needed to learn the lesson of the experience I was involved in. **GOD IS** infinite patience. What I have learned, what I have come to believe without a doubt, is that we are all the equal children of the First Cause. Our actions and experiences don't define us, they inform us. Only Spirit defines us.

Start seeking God's will in your life in any fashion you feel guided to and watch your life change. If I can turn my life around so can you. What are you waiting for?

GOD IS

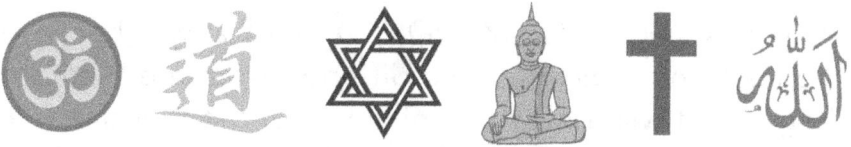

THE GOD TRILOGY

Book 1 is titled *"GOD IS"*; subtitled *"And I thought It Was All About Me, The Gospel of Rev. Phil"*. *"GOD IS"* is my Spiritual Autobiography. Its purpose is to provide you with the basis of believing that there is a Power greater than yourself that is not only watching over you but is willing and capable of intervening in your life for your betterment. This is a spiritual story not a religious one. The journey I will share with you is my own. It starts with an abusive, dysfunctional childhood which leads to a chaotic, anger filled, toxic adulthood. Due to interventions by a Deity I didn't even believe in, I not only survived my self-destructiveness I was able to turn my life around. This process connected me with a few unbelievable teachers and many cherished guides. What I learned along the path I document in this autobiography. I'll share with you my lessons and understandings, my Gospel, and cover the subjects of karma, God's grace, charity, mercy, true spirituality and above all, unconditional love. My hope is that this volume will stimulate you to seek out the source and inspiration of my transformation in your own life.

Book 2 is titled *"GOD REALIZATION."* *"GOD REALIZATION"* looks at the current state of religion and why I believe it is a broken concept. The impact of marketing a non-quantifiable product is explored. *"GOD REALIZATION"* will provide the reader with a Vedic concept known as Yuga, The Cycle of Ages and how that dynamic impacts the various religious traditions. *"GOD REALIZATION"* will look at why I believe the Eastern religions are so different from the Western religions. It will assess the influence of the foundational hunter-gatherer culture on the Abrahamic traditions. *"GOD REALIZATION"* will also, above all else, provide an alternative to the perceived problem. *"GOD REALIZATION"* is mainly a how-to guide that directs you in the process of reaching and connecting with the Divine Presence in your being, which is the proposed solution to the problems presented in the first part of the book. This guide is based on the 12 Step model but is structured to lead you to a deeper level spiritual connection than the traditional, behavior modification oriented, 12 Step programs. This book includes worksheets for each of the Steps and an interpretation of the 12 Traditions that will allow you, the reader, to form your own supportive spiritual fellowship.

Book 3 is titled *"GOD HEALS"*. Having been introduced to and then embracing the Divine Presence within yourself, as revealed in book 1, *"GOD IS,"* and then by following the guidance provided in book 2, *"GOD REALIZATION,"* you have made Spirit the guiding force in your life. We are then led to ask the question, "what do I do with this realization"? *"GOD HEALS"* provides one important answer to that question. It will look at how a deep belief in The Creator has been used not only to control one's body but to heal individuals with life threatening physical and mental disorders. This volume will review healing practices throughout the course of time and provide firsthand accounts of individuals applying spiritual beliefs and practices to facilitate their own ailments.

LOVE & LIGHT,
Rev. Phil

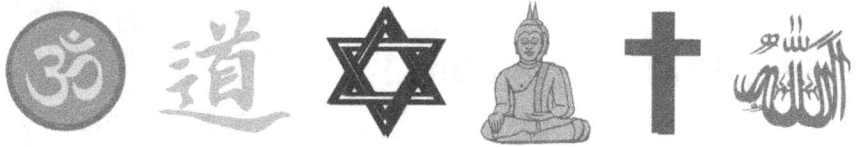

THE COMPANION TO THE GOD TRILOGY

God Speaks is the fourth book in this series, and is a Companion to the God Trilogy. Buddha, in the Dhammapada (The Path of Eternal Truth), as translated by J. Richards, Chapter 6, "The Wise", Paragraph 5, is quoted as saying "As a deep lake is clear and calm, so the wise become tranquil after they listened to the truth." In the New Testament, the King James Bible version, The Gospel According to Saint Mark, Chapter 4, Verse 9, Jesus is quoted as saying "He that hath ears to hear, let him hear." Buddha and Jesus both asked their disciples to heed their teachings, to grow in Spirit. Spirit is like any muscle in the body. If you use it, it grows stronger. If you don't use it, it atrophies. *"GOD SPEAKS"*, was written with the sole purpose of being a spiritual muscle builder. This book contains a spiritual teaching for each day of the year. To further aide you, each teaching will have a contemplative commentary accompanying it. In "The Bhagavad Gita" (The Song of the Lord), as translated by Edwin Arnold, Chapter 18, "Of Religion by Deliverance and Renunciation", Paragraph 19, Lord Krishna imparts to Arjuna "Listen! tell thee for thy comfort this."

ENJOY MORE FROM REV. PHIL!

GOD REALIZATION: LEARN TO LISTEN TO THE VOICE OF LOVE
The God Trilogy – Book 2

GOD REALIZATION looks at the current state of religion and why I believe it is a broken concept. The impact of marketing a non-quantifiable product is explored.

GOD HEALS: THE POWER TO HEAL IS WITHIN
The God Trilogy – Book 3

GOD HEALS will look at how a deep belief in The Creator has been used not only to control one's body but to heal individuals with life threatening physical and mental disorders.

GOD SPEAKS: "IN THE BEGINNING THERE WAS THE WORD..." OM
The God Trilogy Companion – Daily Contemplations

Buddha, in the Dhammapada (The Path of Eternal Truth), is quoted as saying "As a deep lake is clear and calm, so the wise become tranquil after they listened to the truth."

Church of the One God
www.ChurchOfTheOneGod.org

www.ingramcontent.com/pod-product-compliance
Lightning Source LLC
Chambersburg PA
CBHW070428010526
44118CB00014B/1956